A
Glory
in it All

REFLECTIONS
AFTER
EIGHTY

By
JOHN KNOX

WORD BOOKS
PUBLISHER
WACO, TEXAS

A DIVISION OF
WORD, INCORPORATED

Library of Congress Cataloging in Publication Data

Knox, John, 1900–
  A glory in it all.

  1. Meditations.   I. Title.
BV4832.2.K585   1985   242   85–11949
ISBN 0–8499–0511–7

Printed in the United States of America

567898   BKC   987654321

To
Carolyn and Charles Huffman
whom I hold always in my heart
Philippians 1:7

Long have I known a glory in it all

Edna St. Vincent Millay

Look, how the floor of heaven
Is thick inlaid with patines of bright gold:
There's not the smallest orb which thou beholds't
But in his motion like an angel sings. . . .

Such harmony is in immortal souls;
But, whilst this muddy vesture of decay
Doth grossly close us in, we cannot hear it.

Shakespeare

Contents

Foreword □ 11

Reclaiming the Past □ 17

April □ 19

Grandchild □ 21

Possession □ 23

God's Folly □ 26

Greatness □ 30

Like a Tree □ 32

In the Midst of Life □ 35

The Last Enemy? □ 37

The Heart's Wisdom □ 40

God's Strange Gift □ 42

On Being Educated □ 45

Education and the Human Spirit □ 49

Faith and Wisdom □ 53

Knowledge and Belief □ 56

Prayer in Our Public Schools □ 62

On Translations □ 68

Creativity □ 71

Evelyn □ 75

The Imperfect Perfect □ *78*
The English Bible □ *81*
Peace in Our Time □ *85*
Means and Meaning □ *90*
Realism □ *93*
Our National Anthem □ *97*
On the Black-White Issue □ *101*
Charisma □ *107*
A Christian Theology □ *110*
A Better Scheme Entire? □ *114*
Forgiving Oneself □ *118*
When Duty Is Doubtful □ *120*
The Grace to Compromise □ *123*
Night-Skies East of Camden □ *126*
Let Not My Death Be Long □ *129*
Taking Death in Stride □ *132*
Hope Also Abides □ *135*
The Last Surprise □ *138*
Christmas and Easter □ *140*
Only to Be Remembered? □ *144*
The Parting Guest □ *146*
Acknowledgments □ *149*

Foreword

IN HIS AUTOBIOGRAPHY SOMERSET MAUGHAM has some
rather harsh things to say about writers who do not
know what they want to say till they have said it, hinting
at least that their thoughts can have little value or truth.
I winced when I read this because I must confess to
being such a writer. But I must also say that I am far
from sure that Maugham's generalization is correct. Is
it not a fact for many of us that although our ideas
may have some vague form before we express them,
they can assume anything like definite shape only when
we put them into words? At any rate, fortunately or
unfortunately, that is true for me. The brief essays which
comprise this modest volume, therefore, represent not
merely the results of reflection, but to a degree the
process of reflecting itself.

The essays are wide-ranging and miscellaneous in subject, as my thoughts in these years of comparative leisure
certainly have been, and are. Most of these essays were
written with no thought of their ever being parts of a
book. No topical relatedness, therefore, binds them to-

gether. They deal with subjects as different in kind as the felt meaning of a line of poetry and the American civil rights movement, or as the nature of human wisdom and "school prayer." They have been written on a variety of occasions and in a variety of moods. Thus, perfect coherence among the essays is not to be expected. I should be disappointed, however, if the reader did not discern among them, as dominant and never far from sight, certain ageless themes harmonious with one another and serving to impart to the collection as a whole something of unity—themes, moreover, of such kind as perhaps to justify, overall, the title I have given to this book.

The order of the essays is to a large extent fortuitous. At one time after their publication in a single book was proposed I searched for some scheme of dividing them into sections or "Parts," with a view to putting like with like. But these efforts always seemed to end, not in enhancing unity, but in accenting diversity. So here the several essays are, arranged with small regard to logical sequence and very much in the order in which they were written or happened at first to fall.

I speak of these reflections as taking place after eighty. This is quite true; all of the essays have been written within the last two years. But this statement does not mean that they are all new reflections, although most of them, I think, could be so described. Not a few, however, are concerned with ideas which I have long had, although new occasions have brought them freshly to my mind and may perhaps have given them a new relevance or point. Still, any reader well acquainted with my earlier writings will undoubtedly hear echoes of them in this volume. Indeed, several of the pieces could be called small bits of previous writing adapted to a new context and so revised that more youthful reflections are brought into line with my present thinking and feeling. In a sense, therefore, these too are "after eighty."

One minor note should perhaps be added. Whenever the word "man" occurs in this book, it is used, along with the appropriate pronouns which follow it, in the primary, the so-called generic, sense of that term, to mean the human race at its most inclusive or the human being simply as such.

JOHN KNOX

Medford, N.J.
January, 1985

Reclaiming the Past

Since Entering Upon My Eighties I have been recalling more "intentively" than before "the story of my life, from year to year, the battles, sieges, fortunes I have passed . . . even from my boyish days." My story lacks the glamor of Othello's: my battles, sieges, fortunes have been of a different kind entirely. Nevertheless, my living through it again has been for me an interesting and sometimes poignant experience, although I should not expect anyone else, even my own sweet Desdemona, to find it either "passing strange" or "wondrous pitiful."

Such remembering is sometimes regarded as a mark of approaching senility and is disparaged accordingly. To be sure, one cannot deny its association with old age. Just as with the coming of spring we are all but forced to embark on pilgrimages, so when winter sets in we are moved all but irresistibly to recall and describe them. But this impulse is not to be dismissed as an omen of second childishness, a sentimental and futile thing, or a cowardly flight from present reality to an idealized past. I have often thought of it so, but now that I am coming under its power, I am considering it with a new respect. I am recognizing, for one thing, that recollection, if it has some order and coherence, far from being a forsaking of the present, is a claiming of the past as a part of the present, thus greatly enhancing and enriching it; indeed, that such remembering is an essential element in that self-knowledge which Socrates was near to calling the whole meaning of wisdom.

As a matter of fact—will we not agree?—it is concern, not with the past, but rather with the future, which puts our realization and enjoyment of the present most at risk. And this is much less likely to happen in our later than in our earlier more ambitious and active years. Is it not in those years that, preoccupied with an imagined Tomorrow, we are in greatest danger of losing, not only our Yesterdays, but Today as well?

April

APRIL HAS COME ONCE MORE, and I find myself thinking again of Browning's "Oh, to be in England, now that April's there." The truth is that to be anywhere when April comes is a happiness to be grateful for, even in that place where, perversely, we often least want to be, the place where we are. I have often wondered why James Russell Lowell, in those familiar lines of his which set the meaning of spring to such perfect music, spoke only of June; surely it is in April, or at the latest in May, that

> . . . heaven tries earth if it be in tune
> And over it softly her warm ear lays.

Soon even the great hills will seem to be vaguely moving after a long stillness. And, not much later, we may hear with the Hebrew poet the mountains breaking forth into singing and all the trees of the field clapping their hands.

What makes spring so welcome, and so significant to our spirits, is that it encourages and supports the feeling in us that the universe is alive and companionable or, to use a phrase from Aldous Huxley, that there is "blessedness in the heart of things." And to feel so is the dearest desire of our hearts. It is often thought that the timeless controversy about freedom and determinism has a crucial bearing on the meaning we find in human life. Maybe so, but maybe not. It all depends upon whether the determinism is a mechanical or an organic thing. If determinism means that man is a mere cog-wheel in a huge machine, it is obviously a denial of all that some of us hold precious and have found true; but if, on the other hand, the universe which does the determining is felt to be living and loving, and man can feel himself to be a part of a significant organic development—like the bough of a tree, for example, or a tree itself planted by rivers of water and bringing forth its fruit in its season—then his life can be seen as possessing both dignity and beauty.

It is not a degrading thing to find oneself to be a determined part of the universe if one thinks of the universe in terms sufficiently exalted. Man does not object to bondage; he insists only that his Master shall be worthy of his homage and service. The human quest is nothing else than a search for something great and beautiful enough for one to feel freely able to give oneself up to it. Man is always losing his heart to something, perhaps to another person or to an art or to a cause. When he loses his heart, he is at last rich and free; when it comes back to him, as it so often must, he is bound and poor again. The really enslaved are those whose bodies are held inexorably by a world to which they have been unable to lose their hearts.

In spring it is easier than at other times thus to lose our hearts and find our liberty.

Grandchild

I AM LOOKING AT A PICTURE received yesterday of my latest grandchild—a picture taken the very day of his birth. I have many happy and grateful thoughts as I gaze at it, but beneath them all is a wonderment amounting to awe. I think, bemused, of what this little fellow has already been through. I think of his origin, so far as we can trace it with assurance (and that is only a small part of the way), in a tiny speck of living matter, of his nourishment and growth in the mysterious darkness, of the time he first became aware, however dimly, of his surroundings and began to explore them, of the strenuous and dangerous adventure he has just now undertaken and accomplished, entering a world so vast, variegated, complex, and so utterly, utterly strange to him! . . . But here he is, this little man, every feature and organ intact and in place, the intricately balanced whole perfectly adapted to his intricately complicated new environment. In the wildest flight of fancy can we conceive of a miracle more miraculous than this? And yet no less amazing and inexplicable, no less wonderful is every common thing in our common life; and we should be able to see it so if we were able to keep this baby's fresh, new eyes.

And why are we not able to keep this naive and truly discerning vision? Why must the wonder of life so quickly disappear? Is it because, as Wordsworth suggests, the heaven we come from at our birth and which lies so closely about us in our infancy is, as the days and years pass, left so far behind that we lose sight of it, except for occasional glimpses—rare moments of insight, which are really memories of a glory we once knew? Or is the rarity of such moments more truly explained when the same poet writes: "The world is too much with us. Getting and spending we lay waste our powers"—particularly our power to sense things as they are in themselves, without regard to any purpose we may find in them or any use to which we learn to put them? Or are both "explanations" basically the same?

In any case, it is undeniable that God reveals to babes what is hidden from the wise and prudent and that only to the extent we are able to turn, and become like little children, is it given us to see the kingdom of God.

Possession

WHEN WE REMEMBER that "the earth is the Lord's and the fullness thereof," we may see something more than a little presumptuous in the way we humans have taken "possession" of it, dividing it out among us, imagining that by some simple calculations and the recording of some figures we have determined the ownership of forest and stream, of meadow and mountain, of landscape, and even of sky and sea. But we are deceiving ourselves; God is not mocked and his true children are not robbed. I have just been reading a volume of poems by Maureen Mabbott in which she describes sensitively and lovingly the beauties of field and garden in the mid-western town in which she was reared. Now I am enjoying a novel by Mary Ellen Chase in which appear similar descriptions of the Maine coast village of her birth and early youth. In neither case would it occur to me to ask the author how many acres of this loveliness she owned. Such a question would seem absurdly irrelevant. It is obvious that she owned all of it. I do not know whether Turner legally owned a single square yard of Venice, but one look at his pictures leaves one in no doubt that he owned the whole city.

If one were asked to name a truly rich man, one could not do better than to name a medieval figure, clad in rags, refusing to touch money and depending on the poor for his daily bread, who indeed "in mystical marriage took poverty as his bride," but who may have come nearer than anyone else has come to being as rich as his Master, who needed to borrow a penny to illustrate a maxim and who had not where to lay his head. They possessed the world because, as its intimates and confidants, they possessed its secret.

These rich men have not been without their disciples, although most of the disciples have followed only afar off. One thinks of Thoreau, who estimated that his life at Walden Pond cost him twenty-seven and a half cents a week and who wrote out of his experience, "Truly, our greatest blessings are always cheap"—a remark which can hardly fail to remind one of Lowell's lines,

> 'Tis heaven alone that is given away.
> 'Tis only God can be had for the asking.

The highest values go by an unfailing reckoning to those who are competent to enjoy them.

Competent to enjoy them—ay, there's the rub. The great masses of the people, "rich" and "poor" alike, are almost wholly lacking in this competence, and no one has it in anything like adequate measure. The causes of this deficiency are many—and complex beyond any possible analysis. For some of the incompetence we ourselves, in such freedom as we have, may be responsible.

But for most of it the causes are beyond our control, lying either in our nature as the finite human beings we *all* are and as the particular human beings we *severally* are, or else in the circumstances into which we were born and in which we must live as best we can. But however it may be caused, this inability to enjoy the beauty so lavishly provided for us, to accept the gifts of love so plenteously bestowed, is the supreme pathos of human living.

God's Folly

ST. PAUL MAY STARTLE US at first with his bold phrase, "the foolishness of God," but one cannot long consider the world God has made, or love it much, and still believe that God is only wise—or perhaps, in our sense of the word, that he is wise at all. There is everywhere about us an extravagance, a profuseness and splendor, which, if it be not proper to label "foolishness," is surely not wisdom. We usually think of God as deliberate and purposeful. We can use such a phrase as "the definite plan and foreknowledge of God." But not only is it futile to ask what was God's purpose in making everything as it is, it is also impossible for us to suppose that he did so with what we would call a purpose at all. We are told that God knows every star by name— this we can believe, for every separate star is the work of his hand. But that God created each star for some use or to serve some end—this passes belief! The stars do not exist because of their utility; so far as we can see, they are there because God found joy in making them. The earth and the heavens cannot be explained as planned constructions, the products of conscious purpose and labor. Rather, they represent, at any rate under one of their aspects, the illimitable freedom, the pure joy, the boundless creativity, the foolishly wasted beauty, of God.

It is interesting, and perhaps enlightening, to think of Jesus in this connection. Sometimes comparisons are made between the recorded words of Jesus and those of contemporaries, or near-contemporaries, like Epictetus or Hillel, with a view to showing that these teachers were quite as wise as Jesus, or possibly even wiser. That may be. Is not the very distinction of Jesus' teaching that it was not wise at all? Why do we listen, as to the voice of God, when he says, "Do not resist one who is evil. But if anyone strikes you on the right cheek, turn to him the other also; and if anyone would sue you and take your coat, let him have your cloak as well. Take no thought for your life, what you will eat or what you will drink or about your body, what you will put on . . . Behold the fowls of the air . . . consider the lilies of the field." Why, I ask myself, do we listen to such words, and listen, not as to merely human words? It is not because they strike us as prudent words. It is rather, I suggest, because they seem to answer, as the more reasonable and moderate words of other teachers do not, to something strange and deep in the nature of the world and therefore in ourselves, who belong to it.

We use the word "prodigal" in naming one of Jesus' parables. That adjective might be much more extensively applied. Jesus' parables are filled with prodigals, and even in this particular one there are two—the son who wasted his substance and the father who wasted his love. The real prodigal is the latter—dividing his living with an unworthy son who wishes to leave home, watching eagerly for his return, running to meet him when he sees him afar off, falling on his neck and kissing him, calling for shoes for him and a ring, and the fatted calf for a feast for him. Was there ever such a prodigal? And what wise reader does not sympathize with the complaint of the elder son?

But there were many other prodigals: the prodigal employer (who insists on paying a laborer a full day's wage no matter how little he has worked), the prodigal Samaritan (whose care for a stranger overflows all the bounds of reason or duty), the prodigal sower (most of whose seed is wasted), the prodigal host (who fills the seats at his banquet table with the poor from the street). We read about prodigal kindness ("good measure, pressed down, shaken together" and—as if that were not so much more than enough—"running over") and prodigal forgiveness ("seventy times seven").

Once a woman anointed Jesus with "an ointment of spikenard, very precious," and an observer prudently said, "Why this waste: This should have been sold and the money given to the poor." But Jesus said only: "Let her alone. She hath done a beautiful thing." The spilled ointment was a symbol of the vast creative goodness of God poured out in such utterly wasteful abundance.

And does not the Cross exhibit the same foolish goodness? Would it not have been wiser to see that love could not follow its own way in a world where selfishness and hatred were so firmly established, that one could not afford to be freely generous in a world so bound by conventions and traditions of religion, race, and class? And would it not have been wiser to recognize that something has gone so wrong with man that he simply cannot receive, or even tolerate, the goodness of God, even though he was created by this goodness and his life can be fulfilled only in the enjoyment of it? Of course, man deeply knows this, but because he is perversely unable to open his heart to it, he cannot bear the thought, much less the sight, of it. It is for this reason that he nails the Son of God to a tree and crucifies the Lord of glory. Man cannot bear to see depicted too clearly or to hear spoken too plainly what his own heart, responding to what is deepest and most real in the nature of the world, tells him is ultimately true. But it cannot be so. For we cannot finally deny what our hearts know and we cannot finally reject what our hearts love. And the Cross, wherever it is found, whether on Golgotha or on our own street, speaks only the more eloquently of the deep, firm grasp God's beauty and love have, and have always had, on our hearts in showing, as well, what brutal blows we have dealt in our desperate effort to get free of it.

But this last we cannot do. For the God who spreads above our heads the glorious night has also set eternity and the infinite spaces of the stars within our very hearts; and we cannot escape our nature and our destiny. Our wisdom must finally yield to the wonder of his glory and our proud strength to the relentless pressure of his love.

Greatness

I Have Always Been Moved by the story in the Gospels
of the young man who "came running," eagerly asking,
"Good master, what must I do to have life?" only to
"go away sorrowful" when he heard the hard—to him,
impossible—answer. The statement that "Jesus, looking
upon him loved him," gives the story an added poign-
ancy. But now, with most of my life behind me, I am
seeing in it, not merely a story, but a parable—not
only a vivid account of a crucial episode in a single
life, but a vivid reminder of an ominous truth about
life as a whole for each of us. We all come to life
running and eager; too often we limp out of it sorrowful
and disillusioned.

It belongs to the nature of youth to dream that one
is destined to some kind of greatness. We dream of
some great and beautiful thing we shall some time do,
something so great and beautiful that we shall know
it was incalculably worthwhile to live just to do that
thing. We look forward to some radiant day which will
catch up into itself and transfigure all the ordinary days

that went before it, some moment in which will be gathered and expressed all we are and all we have it in us to be. But as we grow older and are progressively forced to recognize both the limits of our powers and the meaning of our mortality, we come eventually, later or sooner, face to face with the fact that we shall never achieve what we dreamed of or even come near to doing so.

In that experience of truth lies one of the most serious crises of our lives. How shall we respond to it? Like the young man, we may go away sorrowful, resigning ourselves to the final defeat of our hopes. But it does not need to be so. Even in this same moment of realization it may be granted us to see that the "life" we dreamed of was never to be our own achievement at all, but God's gift, and that he is still freely offering us all the "greatness" our hearts can hold.

"As the marsh-hen secretly builds on the watery sod,
Behold I will build me a nest on the greatness of God.
I will fly in the greatness of God as the marsh-hen flies
In the freedom that fills all the space 'twixt the marsh and the skies.
By so many roots as the marsh-hen sends in the sod
I will heartily lay me ahold on the greatness of God."

Like a Tree

WHEN ST. JOHN WRITES, "The law was given by Moses, but grace and truth came through Jesus Christ," he expresses, if not the whole essential meaning of Christ, certainly a truly distinctive and very important part of it. Right living is the ideal of the law; graceful and appropriate living is the richer ideal of Jesus. True goodness, as he saw it, was not the dead product of mere legal rectitude, but the vital fruitage of a new kind of life.

It is not difficult to suggest by analogy what this life is, although its essential nature is as mysterious as life is in its every manifestation. Whence, for example, comes the thoroughly adequate potency of the tree, whose great branches bend above my window as I write? How can it be so graceful and strong when it appears to put forth not the slightest effort to become so? The answer, of course, is that it belongs to nature; it is so related to the universe as to be a perfect channel for its own life-force. A cosmic power flows through it. It has life: that is, it is in harmony with nature; its processes are quickened and sustained by a power outside itself. . . . But I, too, am a part of the universe. Why can it not be so with me?

There would be a marvelous sense of fulfillment, a marvelous peace, in such an experience, if it could be given me to have it—a peace consisting, not in aloofness from the world, but in a deeper harmony with it, not in escaping life's responsibilities, but in having something within me, something vital, strong, and joyous, to bear my obligations for me. I should have cast my cares on him who "holds the whole world in his hands." The universe would carry my burdens. Havelock Ellis, after telling of this discovery in his own experience, writes:

> . . . . The dull aching tension was removed . . . and my whole attitude toward the universe was changed. It was no longer an attitude of hostility and dread, but of confidence and love. My self was one with the Not-Self, my will with the universal Will. I seemed to walk in light; my feet scarcely touched the ground; I had entered a new world. . . . Henceforth I could face life with confidence and joy, for my heart was at one with the world and whatever might prove to be in harmony with the world could not be out of harmony with me.

I cannot read this description of Ellis's experience without thinking of an experience of my own. And although it occurred long ago and I have several times tried to describe it, I cannot refrain from speaking of it again. It was a glorious midnight in spring, and I was walking alone along a deserted country road. The air was clear of mist and cloud. There was no moon and the wide sky was brilliant with stars. Suddenly there broke in upon me with overwhelming power a realization of the glory and sheer immediacy of God. I felt an indescribable ecstasy and an almost incredible peace. The whole silent world about and above me became one mighty music, a vast exquisite harmony of sound. I had not needed to ask, "Who art thou, Lord?" I did not doubt that God had made himself known to me in the world itself as its most real and manifest fact—a fact so real and manifest that for the moment nothing else could be known at all.

Such experiences, whenever or to whomever they occur, are in their full glory essentially momentary. "This muddy vesture of decay doth grossly close us in," and we cannot long escape the limits it imposes. But once heard, if only for an instant, the heavenly harmony cannot be altogether silenced in the heart. One has had at least a moment's experience of what it means to be at one with the universe and with oneself as a part of it, and one's life afterward can never be just as it was before.

In the Midst of Life

As I Have Grown Older, I have found what to me has been fresh meaning in the first line of the first paradigm we all learned in our first lesson in logic, "All men are mortal." I am recognizing with a new clarity that to speak of our mortality is not to speak of something waiting for us at the end of our existence; it is a way of speaking of our existence itself. Man *is* mortal—the statement is not about his future, but about his nature. With birth he begins to live; he also begins to die. The upward line on which he rises in his youth is not a straight diagonal pointing toward infinite heights, but is a curve whose trajectory, even from the beginning, carries in itself the certainty of its falling again to the earth.

This is true, of course, for all living things—it is the pathos of all nature. But for man it is true in a unique sense. For him it is not simply an external, objective, a merely "factual" fact; it is an inner, existential fact. For among God's creatures man alone, so far as we know, is aware of his mortality. To be sure, a certain "will to be" seems to exist in all of nature. Even a stone, by its resistance to shattering and erosion, has been said to manifest the presence of this "will," which, quite obviously, is operative in every conscious creature's struggle against threatened destruction. And it might plausibly be argued that this "will to be" implies some dim apprehension of death. But the apprehension, such as it may be, can hardly be called real awareness. And it can still be said that, so far as we have any evidence, man alone in all creation is fully conscious of his mortality. Not only is he dying; he knows that he is.

That knowledge belongs essentially to human existence and indeed has much to do with determining its distinctive character. How different it would feel to be a living person if the sure knowledge of our mortality should suddenly disappear—disappear not only from our thoughts, but from our dreams, not only from our conscious minds, but, with all its deep roots, from our hearts as well! Would not human existence become a different thing? Whether better or worse we will not say, but surely unimaginably different. For in our existence, as it is, life and death are inextricably intertwined. One cannot know the one without the other. One cannot know human life, its peculiar poignant quality, without constantly knowing also, whether always consciously or not, the immediacy of death and its ultimate inevitability.

Not only, then, does man know that he is mortal; he would not know how it feels to be man if this were not true.

The Last Enemy?

St. Paul, In a Notable Passage, speaks of death as "the last enemy." He does so in the context of a world-view radically different from our own, and his meaning, therefore, we can only partly understand. But in *this* we can both understand and feel with him: *Death is an enemy*. Our abhorrence and fear of it, our resistance to it, our efforts to put away even the thought of it—all of this clearly marks it as such. This hostility to death seems to lie deeper in us than in our conscious selves—our very bodies feel it. A shrinking from death belongs to the nature of all living things; and man, even at his most rational, is not free from this instinctive aversion and dread, indeed far from it.

But even at our *least* rational, we can hardly fail to recognize grounds for a reasonable challenge to Paul's assertion. In so far as we are able to consider death coolly and objectively, apart from particular instances of it and in its relation to "this scheme of things entire," we see that it may wear a very different guise and appear not as an enemy at all. For how could there be life as we know it—and it is by no means clear that we would want it to be basically different—unless there were also death. I was rejoicing earlier in these pages in the birth of my grandchild, but grandchildren could not be born if grandfathers were not destined to die. There could not be evolution in nature or history among men if it did not belong to the nature of things that one generation should, not only follow another, but also replace it. Death thus belongs to the basic pattern of the world. And to find that pattern to be on the whole good, as I believe we do, is to see that death—when looked at in the large, so to speak—is also good.

Needless to say, we cannot always thus look at it. To one who is dying, death comes as a very particular, an intimately personal, thing; and in that moment he cannot be expected to look at it "in the large." Neither can those who have loved him and are suddenly bereft. But can it not be said that even these bereaved ones, particular and unique as this death is to them, can often later think of it gratefully? This is true when to someone weary with years death comes as gently as twilight deepens into night, or when to someone suffering unassuageable pain death brings surcease and rest, or when death mercifully shortens the term of someone's enslavement to a disabling and incurable disease. And obviously there are other situations in which death brings healing and peace—indeed, *that* healing and peace, permanent and complete, which only death can bestow. Under circumstances like these, one cannot long regard death as an enemy.

And aside from all such considerations, we should be able to see that, even from the individual's point of view, it is good that human beings are destined to die. If by some miracle I as an individual were granted immunity from death, as the gods granted it to Tithonus, and even if, unlike Tithonus, I should also be granted immunity from all the discomforts and disabilities of aging—even so, must I not recognize that continuing earthly existence would at length become to me an intolerable burden? If the body were able to bear it, the mind could not. I often think of how unhappy and lost my father would be if, well over a century after his birth, he were still alive, no matter how alert his mind and how good his physical health might be. For we are not quite so individual as we sometimes suppose. We belong to our generation, and in our deepest hearts we do not want ourselves or our loved ones to live beyond it.

The Heart's Wisdom

ST. PAUL, again speaking of human death, says, "Behold, I show you a mystery." And so he does—a mystery. No one who thinks seriously about the ultimate meaning of life and death can show us anything else. For all our technical knowledge, we know only the surface of things; all else is mystery and will always be. Paul writes elsewhere, "We know in part"—and we might add, in very small part indeed. But the mystery does not present itself to our minds as a mere void which further research and reflection will enable us to fill, but as an impenetrable veil fixed between our being and the meaning of our being. Although we cannot pierce the veil, neither can we escape a feeling amounting to knowledge that beyond it, or hidden within it, is the creative Source of our being, the Author of all good, and in that knowledge we can find all the solace and hope we really need.

We are enabled to see that our dying, for all its grim reality and critical importance, is only an incident in our living—our living in an infinitely vaster world than the world we commonly see; that heaven and earth are not two separate, much less remotely distant places, but are fused in one continuum. Do we not constantly live with a haunting consciousness of a divine and ultimately fulfilling Reality intimately near and yet beyond our senses' grasp or even our minds' reach, a height just higher than our own, a depth just deeper? And do we not in ecstatic moments have actual glimpses of its glory? Only the limits of our capacity for experience set the narrow limits of our spiritual horizons, just as only the shortness of our vision creates the overarching sky. Is this mere wishful thinking? No, it is not. It is, to be sure, the *heart's* thinking—or, rather, it is thinking which takes fully into account, as our thinking often fails to do, what the heart *sees* and *knows*.

If we can so bend our pride as to yield ourselves to this deeper wisdom, God may grant us to see that what appear to be our little lives rounded by a sleep are, in reality, large with meaning and that their ends, as their beginnings, lie in the unimaginable distances of his boundless life.

God's Strange Gift

When St. Augustine wrote in his *Confessions,* "Thou hast made us for Thyself and we are restless till we rest in Thee," he was expressing the religious meaning of the word "God" as truly as he was defining the ultimate need of man. For it is not too much to say that God is, by definition, That in which alone we can find ultimate repose. The word may have a different meaning for our *minds,* but not for our hearts, where alone we touch the reality of God if we consciously touch it at all (as indeed we do, whatever our minds may say about it). Now, repose, *all* repose, consists largely in a yielding, a giving in, a belonging. And the ultimate repose is a *complete* yielding, a final surrender, not of our bodies and minds only as in sleep or death, but of our very hearts.

"Fear not, little flock," said Jesus to his disciples in a tender moment, "it is your Father's good pleasure to give you the kingdom." But the kingdom to be given was not a sovereignty they would possess, but a sovereignty to which they would be subject. What was prom-

ised was not the privilege of ruling, but the privilege
of being ruled. It may seem strange to say that God's
greatest gift to us—and a gift which only God can give—
is not dominion but discipleship, not ownership but de-
pendency, not freedom but a yoke, not power but servi-
tude. But so it is.

Strange as such a divine Goodness may seem, however, it is no stranger than our human want, which is
more urgent to be possessed than to possess. Sometimes
we talk of freedom and power as though we really desired
them; actually our whole restless life as human beings
is an effort to escape them. We want most not to be
the master of many things, but to be the slave of the
one thing worthy, and therefore alone able, to rule us.
Thus, Jesus once said to an unhappy man who possessed
many things, "One thing you lack," and to an unhappy
woman who was doing many things, "One thing is need-
ful." And in both cases what was missing was not a
new possession or a new accomplishment, but a new
devotion. God's uniqueness does not consist in the fact
that he alone is able to give us all we wish but in the
fact that he alone is able to take all we need to give.
This, it may be said again, is what God most essentially
is—the One to whom it is our nature to belong and
therefore whose service is perfect freedom. We are
bound till he lays his strong hand on us and poor till
he claims all we have.

This is the freedom, the riches, the life God offers
us. He offers us his kingdom—that is, he offers so to
possess and rule us that our feverish activity would
give way to the working in us of his power, our guilty
shame to his forgiveness, our anxieties to his peace.

We should no longer be troubled by constant fears for our security or incessant hurts to our pride. For he offers in possessing us to take on himself the burden of our sins and failures, and in ruling us to carry all our cares. If we were able fully to accept his offer, our life would no longer be ours, whether to manage or hoard or defend: we should have given it to God— but only to discover that in having thus surrendered it, we at last and for the first time really possess it; that in having thus died to ourselves, we at last and for the first time know what it really means to be alive.

On Being Educated

A FRIEND AND I—both of us educators, he still active and I retired—were recently discussing the meaning of education. In the course of our conversation we thought of A. N. Whitehead's essay on the subject, in which he defines the primary and most important aim of education as being the acquisition of culture, which in turn he defines as activity of thought, sensitiveness to beauty, and humane feeling—adding, as we recalled, that accumulations of information had little, if anything, to do with it. Assuming, at least tentatively, the truth of these definitions, we went on to consider how well our own educational practices and those of our institutions conformed with them, especially as regards the basic matter of culture.

A reliable clue to what educators regard as essential, one might reasonably suppose, is to be found in the requirements they make for graduation, the principal one of which is the passing of the examinations they set. Suppose we follow this clue a little way. Will not a survey of examinations leave us with the impression

that educators, by and large, are most concerned about
the amount and accuracy of a student's information,
the very matter which, according to the definition, is
almost entirely irrelevant? Indeed, if we accept that
definition, would we not need to conclude that many
an illiterate person is more "cultured"—and, therefore,
in the most important sense, better educated—than
many a university graduate? And having had no little
experience with both, I am led to think that this conclusion would in fact be true. Certainly the possession of
a university degree is no guarantee that one is an educated person if sensitivity to beauty and humane feeling
are essential marks of such a person. And so long as
the passing of our written examinations is the chief
requisite for the degree, how could it be otherwise?
As for activity of thought, one must grant that ways
of thus testing a student, especially in subjects like logic
or mathematics, come readily to mind; but how shall
we go about determining in this way how sensitive to
beauty a student is or how humane are his or her feelings?

Even as regards activity of thought, one may wonder
whether it has priority over a knowledge of facts in
the actual testing process. If one is to judge from obser-
vation of many college and university graduates, it does
not. Accurate *knowing*, generally speaking, appears to
be esteemed more highly than active and coherent *thinking*. I do not mean to derogate one whit from the importance of the knowing of certain facts as a requisite part
of many kinds of scholarly endeavor; facts may be the
necessary "food" for thought. And, most surely, I do

not mean to disparage a lively *desire* to know for the sake of knowing. A passion for knowledge—the kind of thing Browning celebrates in "The Grammarian's Funeral"—I would recognize as being an indispensable and vital part of "activity of thought." But where in the institutional educational process is this passion tested or measured? Defenders of the Ph.D. program may answer with a reminder of the dissertation which a successful candidate must have written. Surely this, it may be urged, involves activity of thought. And so perhaps it usually does, but not always or necessarily. I have read dissertations which were simply accumulations of data presumably not previously known. In fact, it used to be true and, I suppose, still is, that the distinguishing mark of an acceptable dissertation is that it make a "contribution to scholarly knowledge," not that it be the product of creative *thinking*. Of course, it could be, and often was, both, but by no means was that always true.

As I think back on my own experiences as a student, I find myself feeling most grateful for my teachers along the way, especially for some of them. Of the latter, a few were professors in colleges and graduate schools; a greater number were teachers in grammar or high schools. But as I think of them, what I am grateful for is in no case the facts imparted to me. If I were challenged to name even one, I should be at a loss, although I know I must have learned from them not a few. But my incalculable debt to them lies elsewhere. It consists in their awakening or stimulating in me the joy of learning, a quickening of intellectual interest, a sharpened sense of the beautiful in nature, literature, and art, and the widening and deepening of my human sympathies. *But on none of these was I tested.* Since the major qualification for graduation was the passing of such testing as *was* done, my having been graduated at whatever level has, it would appear, no *necessary* relation to how well educated I was, or am.

Education and the Human Spirit

I HAVE JUST BEEN READING an essay on higher education which has greatly moved and encouraged me. It was written by a younger member of "the academy," whose name, Barbara A. Mowat, I had not heard before. If I live a few years more, however, I shall expect to hear again, for she is manifestly a person of great competence and with many gifts of perception and understanding— besides being a most excellent writer.

The essay would have impressed me simply by virtue of its intrinsic merit, but it had a special interest and significance for me because it was originally an address delivered at a meeting of a society of which Barbara Mowat is a loyal and influential member and with which I once had a close relationship. This society was named "The Council on Religion in Higher Education" and was founded early in this century by Professor Charles Foster Kent of Yale University. Its purpose was definite and unique. Professor Kent was alarmed by the already growing cleavage between the Academy and the Church or Synagogue. He wished to check the trend by seeking out intellectually able young men and women who shared his religious commitment, who looked forward to careers in college or university teaching and who needed financial help in securing the necessary post-graduate education. The Society, besides providing what assistance it could of this kind, would have the great value of making possible a fellowship of kindred minds, with the mutual support, encouragement, and stimulation such an association would mean for its members. The uniqueness in Kent's project lay in the fact that the Society's help of both kinds should go, not merely to persons who planned to teach in religion departments, or even chiefly to them, but also to prospective teachers of history, literature, the sciences, and so on. "Religion" was by no means a sectarian or departmental thing. Its relevance was as wide as human life and thought.

Looked at in retrospect, Professor Kent's project as he thought of it was doomed to failure in the long run (or perhaps one should say in the "short long run," for it is still too early to make a long-range judgment). The secularist forces, which always threaten religion-oriented education, had become too powerful to be overcome or even to have their advance significantly slowed and, as always happens in such cases, soon penetrated the citadel itself. The Society found its original name, containing the word "religion," no longer acceptable. It became "The Society for Values in Higher Education."

This history is requisite to an understanding of the significance and encouragement I found in Barbara Mowat's essay. It reflects her misgivings—misgivings both enlightened and enlightening—about the secularized and secularizing character of higher education in the contemporary world. She speaks of the dangers of the absolutization of relativism, providing, as the latter does, no firm foundation for our "values." But the principal source of her grave apprehensions is "the banishment of the supernatural from the academy—and the use of the academy to banish the supernatural." She uses the word "supernatural" in the sense, not of a realm separated from the "natural," but of a character of the natural itself. The total and indivisible Reality of which we are a part has an innate numinous quality, which we can ignore only with great loss.

> A world, [she writes] in which the religious impulse is suspect and the numinous given short shrift tends to be a sterile world, cut off from many sources of nourishment to the human spirit— given, in such a world, that there's such a thing as the human spirit. . . . As the numinous is banished by the skepticism and logic of human reason, the symbolic dimension of life— that which gives life its meaning—seems to disappear as well. The result is that we see around us—students and colleagues adrift and apathetic; many professors, cut off from the value dimensions of their disciplines, driven to defend their very disciplinary vocations in reductive, pragmatic, utilitarian terms; and, worst of all, the religious impulse, thwarted of a proper object, lusting after strange gods.

All I can hope to have done in quoting and writing is to impart some impression of the rich content of this essay. At no point would I want the writer not to have said what she has said, and in only one respect would I wish that she had said more. She places great emphasis upon the importance of the individual student and upon education's responsibility for encouraging and, if possible, assisting him to realize his full stature as the unique individual he is. This emphasis cannot be too strongly made. But I rather wish the writer had also something more definite to say about the importance of a religious tradition and about education's responsibility for preserving, correcting, and enriching it. Can "religiousness" endure apart from some "religion"? Can "the religious" survive in the absence of a religiously oriented culture?

Faith and Wisdom

A DANGER CONFRONTING THE CHURCH, perhaps in every age but certainly in our own, is that of trying to make its faith more acceptable (and maybe to enhance its prestige!) by bringing it completely under the aegis of a secular intellectualism. Speaking generally, we may say that Christianity, especially in its most creative epochs, has always maintained a vigorous intellectual life; it has nurtured and honored science and philosophy and in turn been enriched by them. Such a relationship is indispensable; without it we fall into a sterile and irrelevant fundamentalism or into a futile and dishonest obscurantism. But except in periods of decadence, the church has never come to the point of acknowledging the absolute supremacy of secular wisdom in the field of truth. It has insisted that in certain crucially important areas what may often appear foolish to the wise among us is, in reality, the truest wisdom.

This was surely true in the primitive church. Christianity began magnificently. It stepped from the soil of Palestine on its westward march with the tread of a conqueror.

It did obeisance to no man. It feared neither the wrath of men nor the wisdom of men. It worshiped neither the emperor nor the scholar. It did not sit at philosophy's feet; philosophy was soon sitting at *its* feet. For all its humble origin among Galilean peasants and workingmen—poor and unschooled—it became the teacher of Greece as it became the ruler of Rome. It did not for a moment acknowledge that truth to be true must pass the tests of the schoolmen. "God who spoke of old times through the mouths of the prophets has in these later days spoken through his Son," declared these early preachers. In the assurance they felt of this fact and all its implications they stood with head high and spoke with clear voice, whether on a Philippian riverside or the Athenian Areopagus.

But in recent years we have become accustomed to taking for granted that man is the arbiter of all things; that "the word of God" is only a rather poetic way of referring to the voice of man's Reason or conscience. We have found ourselves looking both wistfully and fearfully toward the laboratories of the scientists—wistfully, because we hoped that they would conclude that Christian faith might be true after all, and fearfully, because we expected on the whole they would not. But that was not the attitude of the first Christian generation. They knew that their message was, according to what passed as the canons of good sense and worldly wisdom, foolishness. They frankly called it such and then went on to prove by their lives that this foolishness was wiser than men's wisdom.

There are a few items of vital faith—very few indeed but decisively important—about which it can be said that every effort to establish their truth by logical reasoning has both of two effects: First, it fails; one finds one cannot in this way prove them (a faith can be proved only in the living); and, secondly, the attempt weakens the force of the faith itself. A religious faith that can be rationally proved does not deserve its name, and the more simple and plausible and easy we make Christianity, both on its intellectual and its ethical sides, the more commonplace and negligible we make it. Christian faith at its best and most authentic has never acknowledged the supremacy of science. It has ever been ready (again, at its best) to take and use what science in its own sphere has been able to provide. But it has been well aware, as science often has not, of the severe limits of that sphere. And as for wisdom, it has neither feared nor opposed it. On the contrary, it has boldly but loyally challenged it to be itself, to be precisely and entirely what wisdom has claimed to be.

For wisdom, unless it includes within its horizons what is disclosed in man's religious, as also in his aesthetic life, fails to be wisdom. Wisdom's true task is to give an adequate and rational account of the world and of the total human experience within it. Wisdom may begin by judging that faith is not *rational* and should therefore be excluded from such an account, but it must end by discovering that reason is not *adequate*. Human experience is too rich to be expressed in the terms of the technical reason. A specious wisdom aims first at rationality and falls short of adequacy. A truer wisdom moves first toward adequacy and discovers a sounder, ampler rationality on the way.

Knowledge and Belief

ATTENTION IS OFTEN CALLED to the wide range of meaning the English word "love" is called upon to cover. The same kind of obligation is laid upon the corresponding words in French and German, although, I should say, in a somewhat lesser degree. A similar situation exists, but only in English, with respect to the word "know," of which we require the work which the other languages distribute between two. We use the same word in speaking of our experience of a concrete reality, as when we say, "I know this person [or thing]," and in expressing our conviction of an abstract fact or truth, as when we say, "I know that this [or that] proposition is true." But it is obvious that in these two sentences, not only does the verb "know" have objects of two different kinds, but also that the verb itself has two different meanings.

This distinction comes prominently into view when we speak of our "knowledge of God." Of which kind is it?, we may ask. Or perhaps we may feel that there is a prior question: Can we speak of *knowledge* of God in either sense? Can we attain to more than *belief* when we think of God?

By the word "belief," as we ordinarily use it, we mean something akin to factual or propositional knowledge but falling short of the certainty which any *knowledge* should have. Thus we may say, "I do not *know* that this is true, but I *believe* it is." The "falling short" may be in various degrees. We believe some facts more firmly than others, or, in other words, some beliefs come closer to being knowledge than others do; and some facts are so sure as to be, we feel, not matters of belief at all, but of knowledge. We *know*, for example, that Columbus reached America in 1492. A question can be raised, however, whether, in the strict sense, we can absolutely *know* any fact, even so well-established a fact as this, unless it is a necessary inference from knowledge of the other, the experiential, kind. If, for example, I am actually watching the rain fall or am being dampened by it, I can unquestionably say, "I know it is raining"; but can I do other than "believe" that fact if I am merely being told of it, whatever the authority and whatever the reported evidence? In a word, I find myself at least *asking* whether there is not an element of uncertainty, however small—so small, it may be, as to be negligible—attaching to any fact or proposition not involved in, and established by, one's own experience.

However that question should be answered about facts in general, there can be no doubt, I should say, that any knowledge we can have about *God* can rest only upon this experiential ground. I recall being taught the three classical "proofs" of God's existence. We can *know*, it was said, that God is, first, because otherwise we could not have even the idea of him; secondly, because the universe must have a "First Cause"; and, in the third place, because of the evidences the universe presents of conscious purpose and design. I have no hesitancy in asserting that none of these "proofs," nor all of them together, have succeeded. Rather, their failure is itself proved—if in no other way, by the continuing widespread presence of agnosticism. About God, even if about nothing else, we can know nothing, not even the fact of his being, unless we have some experience of God himself.

That it is given to us as human beings to have such knowledge of him admits of no doubt. Not only *can* we have it; we normally *do* have it. One cannot be fully and truly human without an awareness of a Depth deeper than one's own, of a transcendent Reality, numinous and ineffable, an Infinite which, as Carlyle somewhere says, "Man, with all his cunning, cannot bring under the finite." It was not a Jew or a Christian, nor yet a Muslim, but a self-described agnostic who wrote these passionate lines:

> I would know Thee, Thou unknown one,
> Who dost lay hold of my soul in its depths,
> Moving through my life like a storm,
> Incomprehensible, and yet kin to me!
> I would know Thee, and even serve Thee!

Who will say that this is not an authentic human cry?

"But stay!" someone may interpose, "You are speaking now, not of what man knows but of what he feels he needs to know. Let it be conceded that man wants more than he has, even more than this world can conceivably provide him. Let it be granted that he wants what can only be called by some such name as God. Even so, a cry for God is not a cry *to* God as to Someone, known to be really there."

But will this contention bear scrutiny? The quoted words are manifestly a *prayer,* and a prayer implies an awareness of Someone's hearing. Whatever our theology or whether we have a theology at all, there are for every human being moments when out of unspeakable loneliness and need, he finds himself crying, "Oh God, have mercy!", or moments of sudden joy when he hears himself say, "Oh God, I thank Thee!"—in either case revealing knowledge of a Reality whose being he may at other times deny. Must not Whitehead have had such moments in mind when he wrote of religious experience as beginning in an awareness of "God the Void"?

But it need not end there, and, as Whitehead points out, it normally does not. Without ceasing altogether to be the Void, God may become "the Companion." When we cry out of our depths, we may find that from depths deeper still he answers us. When we reach the limits of our strength and sight and if, realizing our helplessness, we wait with hope, he whom we have known only in the measureless immensity of our need may reveal himself as a saving Presence.

This is surely one meaning of the Cross and the Passion. For Christ's suffering is our human suffering in its whole wide range, a sharing without any holding back in the entire gamut of human wants, not excluding this agonizing need of God. It was he who "offered up prayers and supplications, with loud cries and tears, to him who was able to save him from death." Christ's sorrow was our human sorrow, even though it was so much greater than any of us will know, or can know— a sorrow so great as to have become for millions a symbol of the sorrow of us all, the sorrow of mankind in all the generations. But in the very depths of his loneliness and despair, which erupted in the cry, "My God, my God, why hast Thou forsaken me?", he was met by the One of whose reality we are never more poignantly aware than when we are most poignantly aware of the absence of it: "Into Thy hands I commend my spirit." And although it is not given to us to share in the depths of Christ's experience of God, whether as Void or Companion, or to know the fullness of either his grief or his joy, nevertheless it is true for us too that if with all our hearts we truly seek him, we shall surely ever find him—or, rather, he will ever surely find *us*. And when he does, we shall recognize that our desire for him was all the while his own loving action in drawing us to himself.

> I sought the Lord, and afterward I knew
> He moved my soul to seek him, seeking me.

In all of this we have been thinking about religious *experience*, not about religious *beliefs*. One cannot help dreaming of how much better the human world would be if Christians, not to say other religious communities as well, had always recognized this distinction and its importance—the distinction between the inexpressibly precious knowledge of God himself which "at sundry times and in sundry manners" he has graciously given us and the many "little systems" of ideas about him— frequently arbitrary, harsh, and rigid—which we have made for ourselves and on which we seem, more often than not, to set the higher value. If, whatever our "religion," we could always have conceived of our vocation as sharing with others what we have been granted to *know of* God and never as imposing upon others what we have only *believed about* him, how much of cruel conflict and bitter suffering our world would have been spared and how incalculably richer in spirit human life would be!

Prayer in Our Public Schools

We Are Hearing a Great Deal nowadays about the propriety of the offering of prayers in our public schools, but I must confess to finding it hard to feel much interest in the lively controversy. As will shortly appear, I am, as a Christian, deeply concerned about the place of religion in education, but I see that matter as involving a broad cultural situation far too complex for any regulation about public school prayer, whether prohibitive, prescriptive, or merely permissive, to have any significant bearing upon it.

My attitude is not quickly explained. I am profoundly sympathetic with what I believe to be the basic motives of the more intelligent proponents of what is being called "school prayer," and I wish that these motives were better understood by our citizens generally—and if I may venture to say so, by many Christians themselves.

The beginning of that understanding lies in a recognition of what Christianity is. If it is thought of merely as a set of beliefs which seem true to the individuals who profess it, there is no chance of this understanding.

But Christianity (like Judaism, or indeed any religion) is, not only more than this; it is something quite *other* than this. Christianity is nothing less, or other, than an organic community in history, a significant social reality, an identifiable cultural presence—in a word, a *people.* There have been long periods in the past when a statement of this kind would have been quite gratuitous and pointless. The reality and presence of the Church— whether in a particular instance or connection, for good or evil—were manifest and unmistakable. But potent cultural forces—the Enlightenment, rapidly developing nationalism, the industrial revolution, burgeoning commercialism, scientific discoveries and their applications—have had the effect of reducing the Church's influence, both by containing and dividing it. And, in destroying its unity and its hegemony, these forces have tended to conceal the fact of its continuing existence. The Church is *there,* nevertheless; and for its members it is no less surely real and important than it has been for Christians of every other period.

Indeed, many of these modern Christians have been brought, by the very events and developments which have reduced the Church's institutional *power,* to a quickened awareness of its *reality* and an enhanced appreciation of its *importance,* because, for them at least, these same events and developments have tended also to reduce the meaning and promise of human existence. Confronted by the threat of nothingness, these men and women have been moved to rediscover and reclaim the cultural roots of their own personal lives. They have been forced to see that they are not the self-sufficient individuals Western men have been inclined to think they are, but depend for their personhood on an intimate participation in history—and not in history in some vague, universal sense, but in particular concrete histories. Among these, they have come to see, the most important is that historical stream which began when Israel began and continues still, the stream to which the ancient lawgivers, prophets, sages and psalmists of Israel belong and, not less truly, the apostles, prophets, scholars, artists, saints of the Church's own past.

Their own most intimate personal lives, their inner selves, have been formed in the matrix of Christian culture; and the meaning of their existence is largely determined by their deep and inextricable involvement in it. Such unity, coherence, directing purpose and sustaining strength as they may know in their personal lives are related, directly or indirectly, to their organic membership in this historical community. Moreover, the same is true of any meaning history as a whole can have for them. In no other stream or strand of history are past, present, and future united for them and given some measure of coherence. For them nowhere else do otherwise innumerable successive or interlocking histories become a single history. Nowhere else do East and West, the most ancient past and the present moment, become parts of one organic development which moves on toward a fulfillment still in the future. Nowhere else do they find any sense of direction in history or any basis of ultimate hope.

I am not now saying that these people are right, but only that they *are*. The Church exists. Despite its divisions, despite the corruptions and dilutions of its quality, the unique human community which arose in the first

century and had acquired its characteristic form and
ethos by the end of the second is still for many millions
of human beings, not only a fact of experience, but
the fact which, above all others, gives meaning to their
lives and, as they see it, to the life of man in its whole-
ness and under all its aspects.

It will be at once apparent that those who feel in
this way will have a concern about education. For education, however defined otherwise, cannot fail to be an
initiation into a cultural inheritance. And if for this
body of people the Christian cultural inheritance has
the overriding importance I have suggested, it is inevita-
ble that they will want to assure, not only that the education of their children be in fact an initiation into this
heritage, but also that it be *chiefly* that. Needless to
say, this does not mean that they would want the educational process to be concerned largely with the materials
of Church history and tradition; on the contrary, they
would want it to be concerned, without reservation or
undue disproportion, with the whole of man's cultural
history and with the whole realm of his knowledge.
But if, for the Christian, participation in the existence
of the Church is a basic desideratum for his children,
if he thinks of this participation as providing the necessary precondition for the child's proper estimation and
true appropriation of all the other elements in his cultural heritage—then, any educational effort must seem
defective, or even harmful, if this priority is not observed. For this reason, the Christian will feel that,
for his own children at least, all education, from beginning to end, should, in principle, be the work of the
Church, since, in modern divided societies, only educa-

tion under Church auspices could be expected to meet this criterion.

Those who do not share his presupposition will not agree with this judgment; but surely it is apparent that *for him* no other judgment is possible. He cannot in good conscience and with an easy mind turn the education of his children over to those who reject, whether by explicit denial (as a few do), by insinuation (as many do), or by silence (as all are expected to do), what is the major premise of all his life and thought. This fact creates an inescapable tension for the modern Christian, in whose environment the means of education are almost entirely in the hands of secular agencies. And, although probably the majority, certainly large numbers, of our citizens do not feel this tension, it ought to be possible for them to sympathize to some extent with those who do.

But now we come to the immediately relevant question. How is this tension to be ended, or even eased, for those who suffer it? Certainly not by the state's permitting, much less by its requiring, a formal prayer at the beginning of the school-day. How can anyone be so naive as to think so? The roots of the difficulty lie, as we have seen, not in our schools, but in our culture, and are too deep and far-ranging for any legal regulation so much as to touch them. What easement of the tension is possible must come through the Church's doing itself a far more effective educational job than it is now doing. It must educate its members, young and old, or effectually encourage them to educate themselves—enabling them to be at least literate (which, generally speaking, they are not) about their cultural heritage and to become more intelligent about what it means to be a Christian in the contemporary world. Only so can it prepare its children to meet the challenges with which a secular culture will confront them. In a religiously pluralistic society the Church cannot expect the state to assume its own educational responsibilities.

This is surely not an easy recipe, or one likely to be adopted and followed. But is there any other?

On Translations

My Experience As a Translator, as compared with that of many others, has been very slight. But it has been extensive enough to make me aware of the major difficulties any effort at translation encounters and also to convince me that some of them are both unavoidable and insurmountable. No translation, therefore, however competent and careful, can take the place of the original for one who seeks the fullest possible understanding. It is largely for this reason that in an earlier epoch, when the classics were widely appreciated, a knowledge of Greek and Latin was deemed an essential element in a liberal education; and it is, in some small part at least, the reason why courses in German and French are still often required in our schools.

The general ground for the deficiency of even the best translation is the simple and obvious one that what is said in one language often cannot be precisely said in another. Occasionally, when a writer or speaker in English uses a foreign word or phrase instead of an English equivalent, one may not unreasonably suspect affectation, but only rarely is it so. Usually in such cases the foreign term is resorted to because no English equivalent is available. An awkward circumlocution would be required to convey—and even then only approximately—what is neatly expressed in a single Latin, German, or French word or phrase. It is also true that certain terms in another language have connotations or "atmospheres" which no corresponding term in ours possesses.

Moreover, it frequently happens that words ambiguous in another language are matched by no similarly ambiguous words in English, so that the translator, wishing to write intelligibly for the English reader—indeed feeling an obligation to do so—may find himself virtually forced to settle on one meaning out of several possibly intended by the author, thus making definite and clear in his translation what is uncertain or obscure in the original. He may even convey in an unambiguous way what the author intentionally left somewhat vague and indefinite. Other considerations could be cited, but these are sufficient to justify the conclusion that translations can rarely if ever be as finely accurate or as fully revealing as the original text can be to one familiar with its language.

Nevertheless, not only are translations, for practical purposes, obviously indispensable; but for most of us they give access to priceless treasures of mind and spirit otherwise beyond our reach. There are undoubtedly corners and recesses in Homer's "demesne" into which Chapman could not lead his English visitor, but, to the latter's wonder and delight, his guide *was* able to open to him its "wide expanse."

These reflections on translation in general have led me away from the objective I had in mind when I began writing—which was to make some observations on the "new translations" of the Bible which are now current in such abundance. The fulfillment of that purpose must wait for another day. One of these observations, however, belongs in the present context. If the English reader who knows no Hebrew or Greek but is seriously interested in the Bible's meaning will take the trouble to compare in detail several of the more excellent of the translations, he will soon discover differences in the rendering of the same Hebrew or Greek text which reflect the several ways reliable translators have dealt with such difficulties as I have mentioned. He will observe, for example, that in Jesus' validation of the law in Matthew 5:18 the clause familiar to us as, "till all be fulfilled," reads in one very competent translation, "until it is all observed"; in another equally competent, "until all that must happen has happened," with an alternative reading, "before all that it stands for is achieved"; while still another translation reads, "until it is all in force." If, now, the reader will take all these different renderings into account—and other examples could almost endlessly be cited—recognizing that the original text must be such as to allow for each of them, he will possess a more nearly adequate conception of the meaning of that original than he could otherwise gain. This conception will, it is true, be less definite and certain than any of the translations if taken alone would give him, but on that very account it will be more nearly accurate.

For the serious English reader this is the principal value of the new translations.

Creativity

I RECALL AN APHORISM of an eminent philosopher, a teacher of mine long ago: "Man makes mechanisms; God makes organisms." Aphorisms have a way of being too neat to be altogether true, and this one, I should say, is not an exception. But undoubtedly it *contains* truth, and perhaps that is all we should ask of an aphorism. Indeed, of the truth of what this one says *explicitly*, there can be no question: Quite obviously, man does make mechanisms and God does make organisms. But, contrary to what the aphorism *implies*, it is just as obviously true that God also makes mechanisms. There are mechanisms, often countless mechanisms within countless mechanisms, in everything that he has made or is making, from a single atom or cell to the human brain and the stars in their courses. On this indubitable fact rests the possibility of every science, physical and biological; and we can reject out of hand any suggestion to the contrary.

But what shall we say of the other "half" of the implied meaning of the apothegm, namely, that man does *not* make organisms? Here there is some room for differences of opinion, but it is my own opinion that we must accept it as unqualifiedly true. Man cannot create life, and I believe it is safe to say that he will never be able to do so. He is able often to set up appropriate conditions for it, and this work of his is important, sometimes indispensable. He can plow and harrow the field; he can plant the seed and water it; but he cannot make the seed, nor can he force it to sprout and grow. In these latter days he has become so skillful in manipulating the conditions of life as to affect, in amazing ways, its length, its quality, and the forms it will take; but life itself is beyond the reach of his science. When we speak, as we sometimes do, of the possibility of man's "making life," we mean only the possibility of his so mastering the mechanical conditions of life as to have grounds for expecting its coming. But even this possibility is merely hypothetical.

Out of such reflections as these, if one accepts them as true, many questions arise. Perhaps the most important of these is: What are we to say, then, of the manifestly living things which man does apparently make and of the manifestly creative actions he does apparently perform? What is to be said of creative writing, music and other arts, creative philosophical and scientific insights, creative human relationships, as in friendship and marriage—all of them apparently the work of human hands, minds, and hearts? Are we mistaken in regarding them as living things? Of course not! But we may have a mistaken notion as to whence the life in them comes. George Eliot, one of our greatest "creators," writes: "After our subtlest analysis of the mental process, we must still say . . . that our highest thoughts and our best deeds are all given to us."

A. E. Housman gives us an interesting account of how his poems were written. He recalls, as an example, how two stanzas of one of his lyrics flowed unexpectedly into his mind, "just as they are printed," while he was taking his afternoon walk on Hampstead Heath. "A third stanza," he continues, "came with a little coaxing after tea. One more was needed, but it did not come. I had to turn to and compose it myself, and that was a laborious business. I wrote it thirteen times, and it was more than a twelve-month before I got it right."

I do not want to press the analogy too far, but the same kind of thing is true in other spheres of life. Man's creative work never seems to be quite his own. Even as regards Housman's fourth stanza, he should perhaps have said that he *tried* to compose it himself, for, it is safe to say, he did not in the end succeed. When after his thirteen drafts he finally "got it right," we can be sure his success was the result of the same kind of inspiration as had written the rest of the poem.

The primary affirmation of the Creed is: "I believe in God . . . Maker of heaven and earth." God is the Creator. We do not begin to understand that statement if we think of it only, or even chiefly, as an affirmation about some remote and unimaginable past or about the universe in its formal totality. It is a statement about everything that lives and grows in nature or in the mind and heart of man. We are at best instruments of which a divine creativity makes use, channels through which it flows.

And so it is with the truest human *goodness*. We

cannot turn to and make it, any more than we can turn to and make a true poem. It cannot be built by the laying of one obedience upon another like bricks in a wall. Love with all its ethical fruits—humility, patience, kindness, faithfulness, gentleness and the rest—cannot be achieved by our efforts or earned by our merit. What we need is a living Spirit we cannot summon, a living Fire we cannot kindle, but for whose coming we can only prepare and wait as Elijah waited for the fire at Carmel. The goodness of love is always and entirely God's giving of himself to us—a gift which remains a gift even after it is given, so that for one to claim possession of it, much less the deserving of it, is in that moment to lose it.

Evelyn

RECENTLY I WAS ASKED what remembered single line
of English poetry was to me most meaningful and moving. I found the question hard to answer. I had no
trouble recalling many moving passages—lines from
Shakespeare, Milton, Wordsworth, Keats and many others—but these passages all had at least the length of
a couplet, and the meaning and power of each line
seemed to depend in a decisive degree upon the line
or lines which immediately preceded or followed it. Even
among these passages I should have found it difficult
to name one out of so many as most moving. But a
single line! Here my difficulty did not consist in an
embarrassment of riches, but in what seemed at first
an absolute poverty. But after some reflection I reached
a conclusion which surprised me. I decided that among
single lines of verse, I was most moved by the first
line of one of Robert Browning's poems:

"Beautiful Evelyn Hope is dead."

I say that this conclusion was surprising to me. Why
should I find moving what seems to be a mere statement

of fact about a person unknown to me and no doubt fictitious? Yet I do. Is it to any degree at all because the name of Evelyn, owing to some dear associations, has always seemed to me an especially lovely name? Maybe so. But the real reason, I am sure, is less sentimental and more substantial. It lies in the fact that the poet has gathered together four richly allusive themes—youth, beauty, hope, and death—thus telling in a single line the poignant story of a human life and suggesting much of the meaning of the whole poignant human experience. It may be objected that youth is not explicitly asserted, but who will read this first line of the poem without thinking of Evelyn as young? And I should find it hard to believe that Browning did not intentionally give her the surname of Hope, for without the suggestiveness of that word the verse would lack an essential element.

A reader of what I have written might say that my feeling about this line arises partly from my knowing the rest of the lovely poem, and this I cannot deny. The first line is followed by

> Sit and watch by her bed an hour.
> That is her book-shelf, this her bed;
> She plucked that piece of geranium flower,

and the last of the seven stanzas reads:

> I loved you, Evelyn, all the while;
> My heart seemed full as it could hold—
> There was place and to spare for the frank young smile
> And the red young mouth and the hair's young gold.
> So hush—I will give you this leaf to keep—

See, I shut it inside the sweet, cold hand.
There, that is our secret! go to sleep;
You will wake, and remember, and understand.

But for me at least much of the moving story, half-revealed in these verses and fully told in the poem as a whole, is shadowed forth by the opening line.

Wondering if any other reader had been similarly affected by it, I looked into my *Oxford Dictionary of Quotations* and found, again somewhat to my surprise, this one line as a separate entry. Evidently, I am not altogether alone; for others, too, it holds in itself recognizable and moving meaning and can stand alone.

The Imperfect Perfect

As an Editor of Sorts, I have dealt in my time with many good writers, with quite as many poor ones, and with an even larger number perhaps who can be only described as indifferent; but I have also had dealings with a very few who cannot be so readily classified. These few have been men and women who could write well and who had interesting and important things to say but whose standard for their work was so high that they could never (or hardly ever) allow an editor to see, much less to publish it. Unless they could regard it as perfect, they could not bear to "let it go." A zeal like this for perfection, an inability to be satisfied with one's work if it does not reach that high mark, is manifestly worthy, even noble; but it can be inhibiting and crippling.

This last remark does not need to be made about some kinds of work. A mathematician, for example, can be altogether satisfied that he has reached a perfect answer to his problem; and a mason can be almost as sure that he has perfectly followed specifications in lay-

ing a wall. Such workers can survey a piece of their
work and, with God, say: "It is good." But a sculptor
or a musician or a writer is in a different case. I have
read—I cannot vouch for the truth of each item—that
Virgil, unhappy with the Aeneid, at one time asked
that the manuscript be destroyed; that Raphael expressed his disappointment with the Sistine Madonna;
that Beethoven despaired of ever writing a true sym-
phony; that Leonardo left what he felt was a failure
on the walls of the Milan chapel. Whether these stories
are true or not, they might be. But these and other
achievers, great and lesser, in the arts and in the sciences
as well, although they have been passionately devoted
to the seeking for perfection and have had the ability
to approach it—even in some cases to get wondrously
near it—have also been able to make a tolerable peace
with failure to attain it.

But that reflection suggests another. May it not be
that a modicum of "imperfection" belongs *as a positive
element* to the very perfection they have sought? It just
may be true that an absolutely perfect thing or person
would not *as a human thing or person* be perfect at
all. In one of Poe's finest tales, in speaking of the beauty
of a woman, he quotes from Francis Bacon: "There is
no exquisite beauty which hath not some strangeness
in the proportion." The word "strangeness" in this context was not meant to imply "imperfection," but it does
indicate some departure from what would generally seem
a desirable regularity, some deviation from the norm.
Sometimes, theologians think it important to ascribe
to Jesus a moral character and behavior absolutely free
from any weakness, fault, flaw, or strain. They do not

see that in making him thus "perfect" they deny to him the only real perfection appropriate to a human being or possible for him. For the finest human goodness could not have its own peculiar excellence if it were flawless—if it bore no marks of human finitude.

It may be that this paradoxical principle applies, not only to the human world, to the character and works of man, but also to all of nature and to God's creation as a whole. There is an eloquent passage from one of the essays of Gilbert Chesterton which I committed to memory many years ago and which these reflections recall to my mind: I still remember some of the phrases and maybe a sentence or two: ". . . In everything that bows gracefully there is an effort at stiffness. . . . Rigidity yielding a little . . . is the whole beauty of the earth. . . . Everything tries to be straight, and everything just fortunately fails."

Chesterton, especially in his later years, might not have wanted this last clause to be applied to the moral character of Jesus (although I am not sure he would not). But I have no doubt that it does in fact apply to the quality of Jesus' goodness, as it does to the quality of goodness wherever it is found in human beings and in their creative work.

The English Bible

THE LECTION FROM THE APOSTLE AT CHURCH today started
me thinking again about the new translations of the
Bible, which are now so numerous and are being so
widely adopted—adopted, not only for private reading
and study, but for public and ceremonial use. This time
the appointed lection was the passage in the Book of
Acts which reports St. Paul's address on the Athenian
Areopagus. Speaking of God, Paul has usually been
recorded as saying, "For in him we live, and move,
and have our being"; but the minister this morning
read, "For in him we live, move and exist." I do not
know from what translation he was reading, but I do
strongly feel that he should *not* have been reading from
it at that time and place.

I have no quarrel with the new translations if they
are done by persons competent in the ancient languages
and also in English, as all of the better ones have been.
In fact, I know that these translations have rendered,
and are now rendering, a great service. A new translation
often makes clear the meaning of a Hebrew or Greek

word, phrase, or sentence, which is obscure in the older versions. Sometimes, as I have earlier had occasion to point out, it makes that meaning *too* clear—that is, it makes quite clear and unambiguous what in the original is neither, with the result that the biblical author is made to speak more intelligibly in English than he actually does in his own language. And about such instances of "translation" a question might be raised. But this happens only occasionally, and I have no hesitation in saying that, on the whole, the better of the new translations are more accurate, as well as more understandable, than the King James, the Great Bible, and other versions of the sixteenth and early seventeenth centuries. Even so, however, I find myself disliking their use in liturgical lections, and I deeply deplore the extent to which they are displacing the older versions in general attention and regard.

I ask myself why I feel so. At bottom, I think, it is because the King James Version of the Bible (as well as, in a lesser degree the Psalms in the Great Bible) must be recognized to be, not only a translation of an ancient text, but also, and most significantly, as a great English classic in its own right. Quotations from it in our literature are outnumbered only by those from Shakespeare; and if instances of biblical phrases which are no longer "quoted" because they have become an almost indistinguishable element in our language—if these are taken into account, even Shakespeare's preponderance becomes more than questionable. It is not too much to say that biblical language, with all its rich allusiveness, belongs to the warp and woof of our English speech. And let it be remembered that when we speak

of "biblical language" in this connection, we are referring invariably to the King James Version, or (for the
Psalms) to the Great Bible, of which it is a revision.
For a knowledge of this great creation of English literary
genius to disappear among English-speaking people, as
it is far on the way to doing, would mean a cultural
loss horrendous to think of. But how can it fail to happen
if we continue to replace it in Church, school, and public
use with one or another of the contemporary translations?

This question becomes more apt when we note that
most of these translations seem often to depart from
the familiar classical readings only for the sake of the
newness itself. This is true in the instance I have cited.
"Have our being" is surely an accurate rendering. And
is it not also perfectly intelligible? Why, then, forsake
this stately and memorable phrase for the commonplace
"exist," thus destroying the rhythm of the sentence and
turning a poetic line into the barest and most uninterest-
ing prose? Why indeed, unless it be of set purpose to
avoid lyrical language, especially if it be also familiar?
The implied charge can be brought with greater justice
against some of the translations than against others;
and, it must be understood, I am not including among
them the several "revised versions," the declared purpose of which has been to preserve the King James
text, departing from it only at those points where faithfulness to the Hebrew and Greek originals or accuracy
in translation might demand.

In my youth we were encouraged to memorize passages of Scripture—passages from the Prophets and the
Psalms in the Old Testament and in the New such pas-

sages as the Sermon on the Mount in Matthew, many of the parables in Luke, the thirteenth chapter of 1 Corinthians; and I am deeply grateful for my small store of those memories, as I am for remembered lines from Shakespeare, Milton, and other English and American writers. But at that time there was no doubt as to the Bible's *identity:* "The Bible" was the King James Version. The revised versions, necessary though they have been, have to some extent blurred that identity. But the new translations, for all their services, threaten to destroy it.

A paraphrase of Shakespeare might conceivably have its uses, but how absurd to think that it could ever displace the poet himself! The analogy is far from perfect, but it suggests what is a real possibility in the case of another, and comparably great, classic of the same period—a possibility which would have seemed, a generation or so ago, just as unthinkable.

Peace in Our Time

MANY YEARS AGO, when our nation was deeply involved in what was soon to be called the Second World War, I was asked to write an article to be entitled "Re-examining Pacifism." Because I had earlier been a pacifist, an active member of a pacifist organization, I was able to state the case for pacifism, not only sympathetically, but in as strong terms, I think, as any pacifist could have expected or desired. But I had long since been forced on what I felt were moral grounds to abandon it. Although the realization of the increasing destructiveness of modern warfare which the then current conflict was forcing upon us made a re-examination of the pacifist position appropriate and even necessary, I had in the end to re-affirm my rejection of it.

Now, however, forty years later, in these grim days, the possibility of nuclear war—indeed, the certainty of it if war on any large scale should occur—places the whole issue of war and peace in an entirely new perspective, and I find myself considering pacifism and related matters afresh and in the light of a political situation widen unprecedented in kind.

No human being needs to be persuaded of the horror of nuclear war. The desperately important question is how to prevent it. I have just now been reading an interesting essay by two authors previously unknown to me, Ronald J. Sider and Richard K. Taylor, on "Non-military Defense Against Aggression." I do not understand the writers to be taking the absolute pacifist position, nor do I understand them to be asserting that submission by our nation to a foreign tyranny is a tolerable alternative to war. I do not think they would go along with Bertrand Russell's "Better red than dead" or that they would esteem it as nobler to yield to enslavement than to resist it. But I do gather from their essay that they believe, not only that there is such a thing as a non-military defense against aggression (here I would entirely agree with them), but also that such a defense can under all circumstances be adequate and effectual. And on this point, with all the good will in the world, I must disagree. I cannot regard reliance on non-cooperation as a practicable policy for a modern nation of any strength and, in particular, for our own nation at this historical juncture.

Few, if any, will dispute the claim that non-violent opposition expressed in non-cooperation can exercise tremendous political power. We do not need to look abroad; the power of such opposition clearly appears in the history of black-white relations in this country. I should say, however, that the success of this policy depends on the presence of two very definite conditions.

First, it is essential that the oppressors in a given case and those on whose support they depend should recognize, and acknowledge to themselves, that they

are in truth *oppressors* and that, therefore, those who
are resisting them, albeit without violence, have sound
moral grounds for doing so. They must themselves feel,
at least to some significant extent, the justice of their
opponents' cause. Gandhi would not have won his long
non-violent contest with Great Britain if there had not
been a large public opinion in Great Britain sympathetic
with him. Similarly, Martin Luther King could succeed
as he did only because the white people of America,
by and large, both north and south, already knew in
their hearts that he was right. He spoke, not alone for
the black people but also in a significant degree for
the white people as well.

The second pre-condition for the political success of
a non-military method of resistance seems to me equally
important, if not more so. It is ability on the part of
the great mass of those under oppression or the threat
of it to understand a policy of non-cooperation and a
willingness to support it at whatever cost in suffering
for them and their loved ones. If it is obvious that
the successes of Gandhi and King were less difficult
of achievement because of a degree of openness in Great
Britain and the white population of America to information about these leaders and to appeals for their causes,
may it not be said with even greater certainty that their
successes would not have been possible at all without
the massive support they had in their respective con-
stituencies?

But if we are thinking more particularly, as we must
be, of our nation's current situation vis-à-vis the Soviet
Union, each of these pre-conditions is as far from being
a reality as the other. For if it is true that the Russian

people, kept forcibly in ignorance, would be immune
to any influence the moral example of our voluntary
renunciation of military weaponry might exert, it is just
as manifestly true that our country is quite incapable
of becoming such an example. For is it not clear that
no readiness to rely only on non-military resistance to
aggression exists in this country except possibly in a
few small scattered circles? And indeed is it likely that
such a readiness will ever exist anywhere unless in a
physically weak nation or in a strong one whose physical
resistance has first been overwhelmed and destroyed?
The examples the writers of the article cite—of Germany
in 1923, of India, of Bulgaria and the Scandinavian
Countries in the brief period of Hitler's hegemony in
Western Europe, of Hungary in 1949—none of these
cases falls outside the two categories I have just mentioned. What happened in Hungary in 1956 and in
Czecho-Slovakia a few years later reinforces the point.

What then should be our national policy as regards
nuclear armament in our relations with the Soviet
Union? It should be, first of all, a policy of vigorous
prosecution of negotiations looking toward bi-lateral dis-
armament. I should welcome some limited *unilateral*
reduction in our armament in the hope that the Russian
government would be encouraged to follow our lead.
But even so, I can see no alternative to the "deterrence"
on which we have been precariously depending, so far
successfully. I am convinced we should renounce any
attempt to achieve military superiority or even to maintain a precise equality in armament. But I can take
this position only because I have good reason to believe
that our deterrent power is, and after any politically

possible reductions would still be, sufficient for our defensive purposes.

Let it not be supposed for a moment that I do not recognize the tragic futility of such a procedure in the long run. But I cannot give up believing that the time will come—and it must be soon—when both sides will see this futility and will agree to abandon the unspeakably dangerous and incalculably costly "nuclear race." After that happens—if we allow it to happen—future generations may be able to see in the advent of the atomic bomb, not the terrifying event we cannot help seeing in it, but the beginning of a new and blessed era in the affairs of men and nations. War will have fallen "of its own weight." And the most fearsome instrument of war will have become the means of its banishment.

In the meantime, however, a policy of deterrence, although it certainly cannot guarantee peace, offers in my view more chance of it than any practicable or politically feasible alternative.

Means and Meaning

MY ATTENTION HAS RECENTLY BEEN CALLED to an old review by Bernard Shaw of a book on the future of music in England in which he lashed out in his characteristic way at the sentimentality of the concern as professed in certain quarters over the people's lack of what we sometimes call music appreciation. After describing the lot of "a laborer's son," brought up half-starved in a "rookery tenement," bullied, slave-driven, taught "by every word and look that he is not wanted among respectable people and that his children are not fit to be spoken to by their children," Shaw continues:

> . . . This is a pretty receipt for making an appreciator of Beethoven. What we want is not music for the people, but bread for the people, security from robbery and scorn for the people, hope for them, enjoyment, equal respect and consideration, life and aspiration instead of drudgery and despair. When we get that, I imagine the people will make tolerable music for themselves, even if Beethoven's scores perish in the interim.

We do not need to agree with Shaw in his suggestion that it would not greatly matter if the scores of Beethoven perished in order to sympathize with him in his main point—that to profess concern for the cultural and spiritual life of man while ignoring his need of bread and of everything that word "bread" stands for is to be sentimental and dishonest, whether one knows it or not.

But it would be equally false, even if less dishonest, to ignore man's need of music and of all *that* word stands for. For that every man shall enjoy a fair and adequate share in the economic wealth of the earth is not the only important thing, although it is unquestionably one of the most important. May we not say that there are two most important things? One is that every human being shall have a chance at life; the other is that life shall be, and shall be recognized as being, worth having a chance at. Means and meaning: "Man shall not live by bread alone, but by every word that proceedeth from the mouth of God." That has always been true—ever since the moment in our planet's history when man took his first decisive step away from the beast. At that moment he began to live, not by bread only, as he had done hitherto, but by words also. *That* was what made him man. And ever since there have been some benefactors who have given him bread, bread to live on, and others who have given him words, words to live by. And if we have to make a choice, can there be any doubt as to which sort of benefaction is ultimately more important? For the means of life are important only because the meaning of life is more important still.

And this meaning of life, to be *adequate*, must be seen as *ultimate*. Words sufficient to live by cannot be merely human words. However uttered or conveyed, whether through spoken or written language, music or other art, or in some other way, the redeeming words must proceed "from the mouth of God" and be recognized as doing so. Our fathers used to answer the question, "What is the end and object of man" with majestic phrase, "the glory of God." In my youth we were beginning to scoff at so quaint and ancient-sounding an answer and were glibly substituting such phrases as "the enrichment of human life," or, simply, "the service of man." But who that has suffered the tragic events of our time is still naive enough to find such answers convincing *if they stand alone?* Have we not learned that we cannot value man much unless we value God more; that without the glory of God there is no glory of man at all? The most important thing about nature is that there is something more than nature; the most important thing about history is that there is something beyond history; the most important thing about man is that there is God— God, who broods like a mother over the troubled scene of man's short days and in whose mighty purposes our failures are overruled and our small deeds fulfilled?

Without such faith man cannot bear to live; with it he can bear and dare all things.

Realism

NOT LONG AGO in these pages I was thinking about
the plight of those who are not able to give spiritual
allegiance to a universe by which nevertheless they find
their outward life rigidly controlled. We can see such
a condition of mind reflected in a greater or lesser degree in many modern writers of English—for example,
Thomas Hardy—not to speak of French and Russian
authors.

But never perhaps has it been affirmed more clearly
and vigorously, described more poignantly and faced
more nobly than by Bertrand Russell in "A Free Man's
Worship." There he speaks of Man's "sure doom . . .
pitiless and dark"; of "omnipotent power," blind and
reckless, rolling "on its relentless way" over him and
all he loves. He sees Man's only possible satisfaction
to lie in keeping his mind "free from the wanton tyranny
which controls his outward life," and in defying the
unconscious, irresistible forces which will soon destroy
him.

Somewhat grandiloquent as the whole passage may

sound to contemporary ears, who can withhold honor from him who wrote it? If the only alternative to defiance of an alien universe is a servile obsequiousness, then let it be defiance every time! If the only victory one can have in life lies in maintaining loyalty to ideals which one knows have no reality outside one's own mind, all honor to him who is able to grasp and hold such a victory! But after all, it is a poor kind of victory. If man is spiritually alone in a universe of such awful dimensions and power, in what words can we describe the utter pathos of his lot? If such it be, then let us face it bravely. But noble as it would be to undertake that desperate task if it were the only alternative to servility before an arbitrary and irresistible Fate, it loses not a little of that quality if it is a gratuitous undertaking; and I cannot but see it as such.

For is it not true that Mr. Russell's insistence that the world about us is sheer blind, unprincipled power, and that man's only hope of a transient happiness lies in his ability to create with his thoughts an ideal world into which his mind may escape from the real world's remorseless, inexorable grasp—is not this far from being a simple (may I not say, realistic?) account of our experience? Is it not, on the contrary, a highly arbitrary account? Is it not true that although there is much evil in the world, still we should not normally assert that there is no beauty and goodness in it except that which we imagine into a kind of being? There are dawns and sunsets, moonlit nights and starry skies, springtime and flowers and the singing of birds, summer green and autumn gold, gentle rains and fruitful fields, not to mention such human things as handclasps and words of love. That all about us is unrelieved, purposeless power is surely not a natural interpretation of human experience. We suffer much that is ugly and baneful, but we enjoy vastly, incalculably, more that is beautiful and good. Who can deny this? And how can one rest in a view of the universe which fails to take account of it?

As a matter of fact, a good case can be made for the view that if, through love for another person, communion with nature, the facing of death—indeed, by any number of a great variety of routes—one comes to feel oneself near to the heart of things, or as near as one can hope to come, and if such a one reacts to this experience most naturally, he will find himself believing in life's transcendent meaning. He will not be able to express that meaning in words or, fully, in any other way, but he will not doubt its reality. He will know that something significant and splendid is happening and that he is playing a part in it.

This feeling about the universe and about human life within it does not mean blindness to the presence of evil—evil frightening in its proportions and devastating in its effects. But it is seen as an alien intruder. Evil is present in the universe, but is not a constitutive part of it. It exists within us but is not an essential part of us. There can be goodness without evil, but there cannot be evil without good. Evil does not belong to the living universe any more truly than a parasite belongs to a living plant or a cancer to a living body. Evil is the negation of being. In so far as it exists the universe as a universe does not exist, just as insofar as disease exists the body as a living organism does not exist.

But the corollary is also true: the undeniable goodness and beauty in the world are the sign and measure of its true actuality, and for one to whom, despite any amount of suffering (or perhaps because of it), it is given thus to know the world, living itself is a fellowship and a sacrament.

Our National *Anthem*

Few Americans, I suspect, are altogether happy about
our national anthem. The fact that no President proposed
it as such till 1916, more than a century after the nation's
birth, and that his proposal waited till 1931 for confirma-
tion by the Congress would seem to indicate that there
was no great enthusiasm for the choice even then. When
I was a boy, we often sang "America," occasionally
"Columbia, the Gem of the Ocean," and other patriotic
songs, but rarely, as I recall, "The Star-Spangled Ban-
ner."

The reasons for our unhappiness with the anthem
and for the country's lateness and hesitancy in adopting
it are not far to seek. Its words are for the greater
part tied to a particular episode in its history—an episode of minor importance as compared with the really
significant events—and only in the last of the three
stanzas and in the refrain is there any more general
reference to the history of the nation or to its future.
Even there the only challenge, or appeal to our aspirations as a people, is that we continue to treasure our

independence, our freedom from foreign domination, and that we continue to be as brave as our fathers in defending it. There is no celebration of what is most distinctive and admirable in our life as a nation.

Besides recognizing these inadequacies of the anthem's *text*, one must acknowledge the unsuitability of the *music* for group, not to say mass, singing. The tune is intricate and difficult and involves a range in the musical scale impossible for most voices. In consequence no one sings, or wants to sing, more than the first stanza and the refrain. We are too much relieved in having remembered and sung so much as that to think of attempting another stanza—if indeed it occurs to us that there may be another stanza. Who is not embarrassed when, at a large public gathering, it is announced that some popular vocalist will sing the National Anthem? As often as not, he or she does so with a swinging cadence utterly lacking in the dignity surely belonging to such a song. Imagine the Marseillaise or "God Save the Queen" so traduced in the presence of a French or British audience! And how absurd it is that an "anthem" should be rendered as a solo, ever or anywhere! There may be a pretense that the vocalist is to "lead" the singing; but the few who join in it do so weakly and half-heartedly and probably only from a sense of public duty. Everyone is glad when the duty is done and the rather embarrassing performance is over. If all of this is true—and, at the risk of appearing to some as unpatriotic, I affirm that it is—one must exclaim: "What kind of National Anthem is this?"

I cannot help contrasting with it what used to be

called—and I suppose is still—the "Negro National Anthem." The beautiful and stirring music of it was composed by Rosamund Johnson and the words by his even more distinguished brother, James Weldon Johnson. No one who has heard a great audience of black people sing this song is likely to forget the experience, and such a one, whether he be black or white, will almost inevitably find himself joining in the mighty chorus, even if only by humming the tune. For the music is as singable and as memorable as the words are deeply moving. It has been my privilege to hear it sung many, many times; and I seem to hear it now:

Lift every voice and sing, Till earth and heaven ring,
Ring with the harmonies of liberty.
Let our rejoicing rise, High as the list'ning skies.
Let it resound loud as the rolling sea.
Sing a song full of the faith that the dark past has taught
us;
Sing a song full of the hope that the present has brought
us.
Facing the rising sun of our new day begun,
Let us march on till victory is won.

Stony the road we trod, Bitter the chast'ning rod,
Felt in the days when hope unborn had died;
Yet with a steady beat, Have not our weary feet,
Come to the place for which our Fathers sighed?
We have come over a way that with tears has been watered.
We have come, treading our path through the blood of the
slaughtered.
Out of the gloomy past, Till now we stand at last
Where the white gleam of our bright star is cast.

God of our weary years, God of our silent tears,
Thou has brought us thus far on the way:
Thou who hast by Thy might Led us into the light,
Keep us forever in the path, we pray.
Lest our feet stray from the places, our God, where we met
  Thee,
Lest, our hearts drunk with the wine of the world, we forget
  Thee;
Shadowed beneath Thy hand, May we forever stand,
True to our God, True to our native land.

It is obvious that this anthem could not be the nation's anthem or even provide a pattern for it; it reflects too specifically the experience of black America. As a nation, we have not trod the stony road or felt the chastening rod. We have not as yet known what in another context has been called "the purging of pain." (I say "not as yet," for the time may come soon when we shall know it.) But even so, there is no reason why we should not have an anthem which is worthy of us (as our present anthem is not) and of which we are worthy (or as nearly worthy as any nation ever is of its highest thoughts about itself).

The words of such an anthem would enshrine all that is noblest in our origin, our history and our aspirations; and its music would be simple enough to be sung and exalted enough to lift our hearts. Such an anthem might play no small part in unifying our nation around a fresh realization of its nature and mission, quickening and nourishing a nobler national purpose and a more worthy national pride.

On the Black-White Issue

Just Fifty-Five Years Ago this year I decided to throw in my lot with the Negro people as far as a white man could, and having let this be known in certain interracial circles (then many fewer and much narrower than they are now), I counted myself most fortunate in being offered a place on the faculty of Fisk University in Nashville, Tennessee. I was to do some teaching, but my principal duty was to serve as minister of the University Church. I was there one year before my marriage and for six years afterward. I was engaged to Lois when the opportunity came and did not accept it till she expressed her glad willingness to go to Fisk with me. Both of us had been born and reared in the South; but she had never thought earlier of such a career and had had no experience in interracial living, and her willingness to incur the separation from her whole past environment—for hardly less than this was involved—I shall always wonder at and admire, as well as the complete way in which she identified herself with our new friends and neighbors.

My years at Fisk I regard as the most significant of my life. I went with every intention of remaining there always. I left because in effect I was forced out. I had been given a temporary leave of absence for study and when I returned found that the position I had been called to fill and in which I had found great joy had been given to another. Leaving Fisk was the hardest thing I have ever had to do, and I still feel the hurt of it. If I had been given any reason to believe that the action in replacing me was owing to lack of confidence in me on the part of my black friends and parishioners, I should have been broken indeed. The President was a white man, but I do not believe that even with him race entered into the issue unless my differences with him on certain policies involving race had something to do with it. Actually, I have never learned what lay back of the matter. No doubt, certain inadequacies of my own were a part of the cause. But so far as I can know, I was never disloyal to the principle that the Negro has the same value, rights, and dignity as every other human being and that human relationships can be as warm and close across racial lines as within them. They may, in fact, other things being equal, be even more rewarding. Many of the friends I made there I still treasure—as I do all of them in memory.

Having described this background, I hardly need to speak of the joy I have felt in the growing strength of the civil rights movement and of the pride I have felt in its achievements. Goals of which we only dreamed fifty years ago are now within our reach and some of them within our grasp. But a recognition of this very joy and pride will enable one to understand why it is acutely distressing to me to find myself questioning any tactic or policy of the civil rights movement or of any section of it. I wish I could agree with every word which every black leader says. My deep sympathy with the objectives of the movement, the knowledge I have of the bitter fruits of segregation, the constant reminders of its continuing presence, and the total revulsion I feel toward racial discrimination in every area of our life and in all its forms—all of this is almost enough to submerge any doubts I may have about particulars— "almost," but not quite.

My doubts arise when any particular policy or statement seems to me to violate either or both of two principles—one, the principle of absolute equality and the irrelevance of racial differences as regards all matters of privileges and rights, political, economic and social; and the other, the principle that there is a radical difference between de-segregation and integration and that only the former can be achieved by law or by force. Whatever questions or opposition a statement of these two principles might arouse in some of the contemporary black leaders of the civil rights movement—and I know that many would, on the contrary, cordially accept them—I feel sure that they would have been taken for granted by men like Walter White, James Weldon Johnson, Philip Randolph, Charles Johnson, and, I believe, though I did not know him and cannot speak with the same assurance about him, by W. E. B. DuBois.

The first principle means that there must be no discrimination whatever on the basis of race, whether against the Negro or in his favor. No policy which discriminates specifically to the black man's advantage can

be a sound policy, and therefore, in the long run, no
such policy can really be to his advantage. It may represent a violation of his dignity even more hateful, for
being more subtle, than any overt insult might be. I
recall with what anger I reacted to a suggestion of a
colleague on an admissions committee at the University
of Chicago, some five years after I had left Fisk, that
a certain applicant with a sub-minimal academic record
be admitted because he was a Negro. I reacted in the
same way when a similar suggestion was made at Union
Theological Seminary some years later. In each case,
my reaction was, I am quite sure, precisely the same
reaction all my Negro friends of fifty years ago would
have experienced—only, if possible, with a deeper and
more impulsive anger than mine. I saw the suggestion
as involving a reflection on the Negro people. What
the Negro asked for then, and what the black man asks
for now, is equal opportunity, the destruction of all
racial barriers to his right to express himself, to develop
and use his talents, to fulfill his God-given destiny, to
enjoy all the good things of life; he did not ask, and
he does not ask, for special privileges and concessions.
I cannot help feeling that when any of his leaders ask
for these for him, they put him in a false position and
put his just cause in jeopardy.

My opinion here needs to be clarified and guarded
at two points. I should not call the action "discrimina-
tory" if, when two equally qualified applicants approach
a bank or a school, the black applicant is chosen. This
kind of reversal of an earlier unjust and unnatural segregation policy is, it seems to me, not only legitimate
but often required. This is not a matter of sacrificing

quality and truth but rather of according a justice which had previously been denied. I recognize also the urgent need of our investing time and money on a large scale in special educational and other efforts of which the Negro will be the largest beneficiary. But this will be true only because so large a proportion of the submerged part of our population is black. The efforts should be directed to helping the unfortunate and retarded of whatever race, and regardless of race. A proposal of a public arrangement to help the black man in his poverty and illiteracy which will not also help the white man in his poverty and illiteracy would, I should say, be unjust and ultimately self-defeating. In other words, any acceptable plan must be color-blind, even though the actual beneficiaries of it at any given time or place may happen to be almost entirely of one or the other race.

The second principle of which I have spoken as basically and permanently valid is that there is a difference between desegregation and integration and that this distinction is of the greatest importance, despite the shameful abuse of it which the prejudiced may often hypocritically make. By "desegregation" is properly meant the removal of all racial barriers, and the offering of all necessary means, to the full and equal sharing by black and white alike in all the common goods; and for its achievement—in every area of our public life, political, economic, social—the state is in the final resort inescapably responsible. By "integration" is meant the sharing itself; and here the state has reached the limits of its power. Integration must ultimately be voluntary, persons finding one another and a common ground. Desegregation may also, of course, be voluntary; but, if it is not, it can and must be enforced. But "enforced integration" is a contradiction in terms and, in practice, the effort to bring integration about by force is self-defeating. Since compulsory desegregation is frequently necessary in opening the way to integration, one may often find it hard to separate the two processes or even to distinguish between them, but they are radically different. One is a mechanical process; the other is organic. We must love and embrace integration as truly as we hate and spurn segregation; but the methods appropriate to achieving the one are not the same as those often necessary in getting rid of the other.

I wonder if anyone in these days who expresses himself, even if only in the most general and basic way, upon this complex issue of public policy, can feel content that he has succeeded in saying just what he thinks and feels. Certainly, I am not satisfied with what I have just written and know that I run the risk of being misunderstood in writing it—misunderstood perhaps by some whose good opinion I greatly cherish or desire. But, if not on what I have *succeeded* in saying, then most surely on what I have been trying to say, I must take my stand. And I believe that in doing so I am in the company of the noblest and wisest of the many wise and noble Negroes I have known, admired, and loved.

Charisma

It May Be a Prejudice of Age, but I confess to feeling some distaste for the word "charisma" as it is now being very widely used. We are being constantly told that this or that politician or other public figure has "charisma" and another has not; and, apparently, it is very important, for every practical purpose, to possess it. Deficiencies in intelligence, in knowledge or judgment, even in honesty, are, it would appear, of small account in determining popular approval and influence as compared with the possession of "charisma."

"Charisma," needless to say, is a Greek term brought into English without any change in spelling. It means, quite simply a gift, a gift of any kind graciously bestowed. Obviously, its current meaning is quite different from this, and one may wonder at first how and why this foreign term with its quite new meaning has come to be a familiar part of our language. Moreover, its adoption appears to be a very sudden and recent happening. The word does not appear in the Webster Unabridged of 1950, but I find it in the Random House

Dictionary of 1966. If so much were not happening to our beloved language, most of it unfortunate, one might be amazed that in so short a time as sixteen years a non-technical term previously not known at all in English should have become so thoroughly acclimated.

This surprise is heightened when we recognize that the term, with a meaning unrelated to its general Greek sense, has arrived solely and directly from the writings of St. Paul and, furthermore, specifically from one instance of its use there. It was Paul's understanding that what we call "talents" (another English word of biblical origin), when possessed by members of his small communities, were not merely natural aptitudes or capabilities but were special "gifts" of God. (Following him, we, too, call talents "gifts.") One member might have received the gift of teaching; another of preaching; another of healing; still another of administration. Even the ability to be useful in some very humble office in the community life, such as the taking of the church's help to a sick or needy member, was for Paul a "spiritual gift," a charisma.

Thus far, there is nothing in Paul's use of the term to give rise to its present meaning. It happens, however, that although the *charismata* were presumably, almost by definition, constructive, one of the "gifts" became the source of serious disruption and division, and caused Paul no little perturbation and perplexity. This was the "gift of tongues"—by which we would understand a capability for ecstatic speech, exciting to hearers, not because it was understood, but, partly at least, because it was *not* understood. This "gift" became disruptive and destructive because those who possessed it were likely to think of themselves as more highly "gifted" than others—as possessing the supreme charisma—and, what is much more significant, because they were likely to be so esteemed by many of their hearers. The situation was difficult for Paul to deal with because his general thesis was such that he could not categorically deny the authenticity of the gift of tongues, but at the same time, seeing the injury its possessors were doing, he could not refrain from castigating their arrogance and deploring their influence. Five words, he writes, spoken from understanding to understanding, are worth more than ten thousand words uttered in what we would call a frenzy.

It is evident and undeniable that the current meaning of "charisma" derives directly and specifically from this particular instance of its use in the Pauline writings. Quite obviously, that meaning has been greatly expanded. But if simple charm in public discourse is meant, why do we not say so? Why do we use a term of whose source in the "gift of tongues" so many of our contemporary preachers and politicians, credited with "charisma," are constantly reminding us? They may have little intelligible, not to say true or useful, to tell us. But they have "charisma," and *that*, it seems, is the important thing!

ᴄᴀ *Christian Theology*

A FRIEND RECENTLY ASKED ME what I perceived to be the distinction between "philosophy" and "theology." The best answer I could give him offhand was that I thought of both as being attempts to rationalize, to make sense of, human experience, but that whereas philosophy was concerned with universal human experience as such, the theologian's concern was also with the distinctive experience of his own religious community. Thus, a Muslim, a Jew, and a Christian might come closer to agreeing with one another as philosophers than they were likely to come as theologians—although, I might have added, I think they could come nearer to doing so than they have thus far done.

This question of my friend reminded me that in this record of some of my reflections in recent years, while I have often written as a Christian, I have not attempted anything like a systematic statement of a theological position. Since I now know that these essays are to be published, I feel that I owe it to myself, and possibly to the reader, to make such a statement, however summary it may need to be; and I cannot do better than to repeat some paragraphs from an earlier writing.

The key to my theology, such as it is, lies in the tendency developed over many years to find the reality of Christianity, the actual, concrete meaning of the word, in the Church. By "the Church" I mean, not something institutional (although it is hard to believe it could have survived, or can survive, without some institutional structure), but a definite, identifiable, historically created *community*. Now the word *community* is, primarily, not a quantitative, but a qualitative term; that is, it designates, primarily, not a collection of people, but a kind of relationship among them. They are conscious participants in a common corporate existence of some kind, be it family, nation, or what not. They are conscious sharers in the possession, or experience, of something precious, peculiar to themselves.

The Greek word *koinonia*, which can be rendered in English as "communion," or "partnership," or "sharing," or "fellowship," is never in the New Testament to be translated as "community," in the sense in which we ordinarily use that term. That sense represents an enlargement of the Greek term, so as to make it mean, not the "fellowship" or "sharing" itself, but a group of persons among whom presumably a "fellowship" or "sharing" exists. Often when we use the word *community* the emphasis falls more upon the fact that a number of persons are involved than upon the shared experience which binds them together. But when we speak of the Church as "a historical community," if we are being at all true to the New Testament meaning of the term, we are thinking primarily of the precious common experience, shared in by millions over many generations, which makes it the particular community it is.

And what is this "precious common experience"? It consists in a common memory of, and loyalty to, Jesus as the true and loving person he was and in a common experiencing of the Spirit as being both the Presence of God and the continuing Presence of this same person—the two "Presences" being, *in experience*, inseparable and all but identical. This, it seems to me, is not a theoretical definition, or the statement of a norm, but is simply a description of what the Christian finds true about himself and has found true ever since the Resurrection (which was itself an inference from the experience of this "continuing Presence"). The essential, overarching, and to the Christian indubitable, miracle of Christianity, what he speaks of as "the act of God in Christ," was God's bringing into being around Jesus of this shared existence, the making possible through him of this shared experience. All the traditional beliefs about the unique "nature" of Jesus, about his "divinity" as different *in kind* from the divinity in every man— beliefs which have been so unnecessarily divisive among Christians and between Christians and Jews—all such beliefs represent our fumbling efforts to explain a unique *event*, which was the creation around Jesus of a new community. And the explanation of the uniquely divine meaning of this event and this community lies, not in history at all, even in the man Jesus, but in him who transcends history but is ultimately sovereign over it and exercises his activity within it. This is "God as known in Christ."

I have never said, though some have understood me

so, that it is *only* through Christ—that is, *only* in the community created around Jesus, remembered and still known—that God is known. Indeed, I have often affirmed that if this were true he could not be God. For in him, "all things live and move and have their being" and he is "the light that lighteth every man that cometh into the world." But I have recognized what it seems to me is obviously and necessarily true, that God is known *in a distinctive way* through the historical event of Christ and in the community in which that event has been perpetuated.

To explicate, as far as possible in rational terms, that distinctive way is the task of Christian theology.

A Better Scheme Entire?

MORE THAN ONCE in the old *Saturday Review*, Norman Cousins, as I recall, affirmed and defended his conviction that in a universe infinite in time and space there can be no conceivable event which will not at some time or place occur in it. If I am mistaken as to just what he wrote, I am not mistaken in the impression I received of his meaning. I remember also that I found his argument unconvincing. Some recent reading has led me to think of it again, and I find myself of the same mind about it.

I have used the word "conceivable" in my summary of Cousins' proposition. I cannot be quite sure that he did not say "possible" instead; but if so, unless my impression is very much in error, he used that word in the sense of conceivable. He would, of course, not have been alone in doing so. Indeed, we commonly employ these terms interchangeably. We say, in some situation, "Anything is possible," when we mean, "I do not know which of many conceivable events will actually occur." But there is a world of difference between the conceivable and the possible. It is certainly plausible,

probably logically necessary, to argue that in a given
actual universe infinite in space and time everything
possible will happen. But not everything *conceivable!*
For we can conceive of events, as we frequently do in
our dreams or fantasies, which are quite impossible
within our universe, no matter how far it extends in
time and space. Some of these we can identify as such,
as, for example, those involving logical contradiction,
but the actually impossible cannot be limited in this
way. In any situation, although we may not be able to
know what is possible, we *can* know that *some* imagin-
able things are definitely possible and that others, just
as definitely, are not possible.

The occasion of my thinking again about this distinction was my coming across, in the course of some general
reading, the oft-quoted statement: "This is the best of
all possible worlds." This statement originated among
the philosophers, and perhaps it should be left there.
Certainly we must depend upon them for any adequate
discussion of it. But who of us can be expected not to
ponder it? I recall that when I first heard it I regarded
it as obviously absurd. How blind to evil, how callous
to suffering, must one be to hold such a thought! How
different, how immeasurably *better*, we are likely to say
to each other, the world would be

> . . . could you and I with Fate conspire
> To grasp this sorry scheme of things entire.
> Would we not shatter it to bits and then
> Re-mould it nearer to our heart's desire!

But reflection makes me less confident that, if there
is to be a real world at all, a better one than ours is
actually possible. Needless to say, a better world in

this or that respect is, not only conceivable, but also possible, and moreover, is constantly coming to pass. The physical health of the world, for example, is being improved; communication among persons and groups is being made easier. Most of us would regard these changes as good, and we trust that many more such goods are yet to be realized. But all of these already belong to our world *as possibilities.* And any estimate of the goodness of the world as a "scheme . . . entire" must take this fact into account.

But, it may be asked, would not our world obviously be better if all these possibilities had been actualities from the start? So it might seem. Yet, is this really true? Imagine, if one can, a world without possibilities of change and growth. Even if by "better," we mean only preferable from our human point of view, would such a world be better? A world without the challenge of an unknown future, without our world's uncertainties and risks, without its anxieties and hopes, without life's promises and threats, its defeats and victories, a world of perfect order but without freedom or even the illusion of freedom—can we really think such a world would have been better? In raising these questions I am far from presuming that I am disposing of an abstruse philosophical problem; I am wanting only to suggest that there may be good grounds for doubting that this "scheme of things entire" is so very "sorry" after all.

The issue, I recognize, must be left to wiser minds than mine. I feel fairly sure only of this: None of these minds will be wise enough to devise an actual world as coherent, as durable, as dependable as ours, or one which, taken as a whole, persons like ourselves would find nearer to our heart's desire. The world we know and in which, despite all the manifestations of goodness and beauty, we find so much to complain of, may be the best possible simply because it is the only real world *possible* at all.

James Branch Cabell once quipped, with seeming aptness: "The optimist proclaims that we live in the best possible world, and the pessimist fears this is true." But it is at least conceivable that neither optimism nor pessimism is relevant and that the "proclamation" is simply a plain statement of the sober truth.

Forgiving Oneself

IT IS IN OLD AGE that we are in the best position to
fulfill Socrates' injunction, "Know thyself." This is true,
not only because it is then that we have most freedom
to seek self-knowledge, with least to distract us, but
also because it is not till then that the data of which
this knowledge must take account are in amplest supply.
These data are the events in our inner experience as
they are remembered and are still occurring.

But these experiences, no matter how large the body
of them, are only the raw material of self-understanding.
They must be gathered together ("recollected"), sorted
out, and their meaning and value assessed. This is no
small undertaking. The recollecting itself, if it aspires
to comprehensiveness, is enormously difficult. We are
often told that in the moment of sudden death the entire
course of someone's life passes before his eyes. We
cannot but wonder how such a fact can be known. But,
apart from this consideration, we know, if we think
about it, that it cannot be true. One's life, even if one
is cut down in youth or middle age, is far too big and
complex for such a vision to be possible.

The store of a lifetime's memories is so vast and variegated that, it would seem, another lifetime would not be long enough for the mere recalling of them; and for the taking stock of them, as the acquirement of self-knowledge would require, still another lifetime would hardly suffice. I am bound, therefore, to conclude that "Know thyself" is one of the many goals to be aimed at and striven for, but in this life never to be attained. I cannot speak for others, but for myself I would say that, among the innumerable perplexities I have learned I must live with, are deep perplexities about *myself.* I shall speak of just one of them.

Why should the sins and follies of years long past seem, as I look back on them, so grievous, so very grievous—burdening my conscience in sleepless hours and often haunting my dreams? Why, I ask myself, should it be so? It is not because I distrust the forgiveness of God. His grace, to which I owe all that is good in my life, is surely sufficient to cover all that is evil. No, it is because I cannot forgive myself. I used to pray with the Psalmist: "Remember not the sins of my youth and my transgressions." Now I am more strongly and deeply moved to pray that God may enable me also to forget them. I say with the great congregation: "Forgive us our trespasses as we forgive those who trespass against us." But I have learned in these later years that, hard as it sometimes is to forgive another, it is often far easier than to forgive oneself.

When Duty Is Doubtful

WHEN PORTIA REMARKS TO HER MAID, "If to do were as easy as to know what were good to do, chapels had been churches and poor men's cottages princes' palaces," she states a principle to which we doubtless find ourselves assenting without question. John Drinkwater in more serious mood expresses the same idea in one of his poems, "A Prayer," in which he pleads, not for knowledge—*this* he confesses he has—"But, Lord, the will—there lies our bitter need."

True as this is, however, it is not the truism we might at first suppose. Although our moral need undoubtedly consists primarily, not in our lack of knowledge, but in the weakness of our moral purpose, still all of us find ourselves in situations where, it seems, doing would be easy if only we could see clearly what we ought to do. To cite one example: In a world where all human beings, without knowing one another or even of one another's existence, are nevertheless tied together so intimately, so inextricably, and, as things are, so inequitably, that my gain means all too often another's loss; my comfort is enjoyed at the price of another's misery;

I profit by the agony of some half-starved laborer on the other side of the planet—in such a world, we often find ourselves uttering the same prayer as Hamlin Garland voices in a poem which he calls, "The Cry of the Age":

> What shall I do to be just?
> What shall I do for the gain
> Of the world—for its sadness?
> Teach me, O seers that I trust."
> Chart me the difficult main
> Leading me out of my sorrow and madness;
> Preach me out of the purging of pain.
>
> Shall I wrench from my finger the ring
> To cast to the tramp at my door?
> Shall I tear off each luminous thing
> To drop in the palm of the poor?
> What shall I do to be just?
> Teach me, O ye in the light,
> Whom the poor and the rich alike trust:
> My heart is aflame to be right.

And the mood of this poem is just as authentic as that of Drinkwater. These are not times ideally adapted to exemplifying the lines,

> When Duty whispers, low, Thou must,
> The youth replies, I can.

But the fault does not lie altogether with the youth. Duty herself has become doubtful or equivocal.

I have cited one example of our moral dilemma, but only a little reflection will bring to mind a host of others.

All of this being true, how can I maintain anything approaching moral integrity? Here, I believe, at least two things can be said. First, I must not permit a recognition of the far-reaching and complicated character of my moral situation to make me less responsible in carrying through any obligation I can more or less clearly see as lying within my power to fulfill. My father, who died sixty years ago, was far less aware of the range of his ethically significant involvements than I have been forced to be of mine; he was not greatly troubled by any number of matters which to me have serious ethical implications. But I am pretty sure that in the somewhat more limited area in which his moral life was lived he acted with greater decisiveness and maintained a deeper integrity.

The second obvious thing is this: I must not let confusion as to how I ought to act in respect to the injustices and cruelties of our social scheme make me callous to their reality. The bitterest charge the prophet Amos can bring against the privileged classes among his contemporaries is that they were not "grieved for the affliction of Joseph." It is one of the marks of maturity that as we grow older we become less sanguine than we once were about the effectiveness of any proposed remedy for the world's ills. But I shall have purchased that maturity at much too high a price if I shall have become less sensitive to the reality of those ills and to the plight of those who suffer so grievously under them or become less sharply conscious of the possible share I have in responsibility for them. However doubtful I may be as to what, in my situation, I ought to do "for the gain of the world, for its sadness," I must not, in frustration or weariness, cease deeply to care.

The Grace to Compromise

SOME WEEKS AGO I mentioned here a passage from one of Gilbert Chesterton's essays which was recalled to my mind in the course of some reflections on the rather paradoxical fact that in all perfection—at any rate, in all perfection we human beings can recognize as such, much less aspire to—there is an element of imperfection, a falling short of what in the abstract would be considered the norm. When the essayist speaks of bows beautiful in their bending and, as he also does, of sword blades curling "like silver ribbons," and concludes, "The cosmos is a diagram just bent beautifully out of shape," surely he has something like this meaning in mind.

But this was not the only, or even the primary, meaning Chesterton intended, as the final part of the passage makes clear. Although it may be beautiful to see the foil "curve in the lunge," one will not want to begin "the battle with a crooked foil." In the same way, although the "strict aim, the strong doctrine" may have to "give a little in the actual fight with facts," it will not do to "start the fight with a weak doctrine or a twisted aim." "Do not try to bend," he concludes, "any more than the tree tries to bend. Try to grow straight and life will bend you."

Not only is it true that no one can quarrel with this "moral," but also that one cannot fail to be grateful to Chesterton for drawing it so beautifully—may I not say, even in this context, so *perfectly?* His words have the great virtue of saying admirably what is undoubtedly—but not too obviously—true, and of doing so in such a way as to set the reader pondering whether they represent the whole truth. I remember Shailer Mathews' offering a definition of the epigram which was itself an epigram worth remembering. "An epigram," he said, "is a half-truth so phrased as to annoy one who believes the other half." Master though Chesterton was of the epigram and frequently as he used it, no one could regard the quoted words of his as conforming to this definition; they represent more than a half-truth, and most certainly they do not annoy. Still, I am led to ask whether they do full justice to the disposition and ability to compromise.

Compromise, especially moral compromise, is *prima facie* a pejorative term. The first demand of rectitude is that a person be true to his own convictions; and any deviation from them in deference to the convictions of others is, to say the least, unfortunate, whether in the intellectual or the moral sphere. But with this *prima facie* view I cannot feel quite satisfied. It is good that the tree normally grows straight, but it is also good that, just as normally, it bends. It would not be the whole truth to say that the tree resists the wind, and, in bending, fails. Why not say, as well or instead, that it cooperates with the wind and, in bending, succeeds? It undoubtedly belongs to the tree's nature to grow straight, but just as certainly it belongs to its nature to bend.

To be sure, it must not be asked to bend too much. There are limits to its complaisance. When these are reached, its bending becomes tense and grudging; and the point may come when it will prefer breaking to bending. But before that point is reached it bends gracefully and graciously, for it knows from its beginning what we human beings have to learn: that "aims" can sometimes be too "strict" and "doctrines" can sometimes be too "strong."

Night Skies East of Camden

A FRIEND OF MINE has written me about a camping trip he and a companion took during the summer just past into a remote part of the Adirondacks. I valued particularly his description of the starry nights, so brilliant he could not bear to use the tent he had brought for sleeping. How well I remember such nights! For a large part of my life, I fear, I took them as a matter of course, but I can recall not a few times when I was more intensely aware. Of one of these I have written earlier in these pages. But as I read my friend's words, I thought also of many occasions during my "circuit-riding" days in the Alleghanies of eastern West Virginia when I would spend much of a night riding horseback through utterly uninhabited terrain under such a sky as he described and reciting aloud some of the Psalms—the nearest human ear being miles away but the stars seeming close enough to hear.

I say I *remember* all of this, for I never see such skies now. There are few nights in good weather, winter or summer, during whose late hours I do not, in a period

of wakefulness, stand at least half a minute outside
our door under the open sky. But at best there are
only a few blurred splotches of pale yellow and these
often seen only with difficulty through the murky haze.
Always I look up half hoping I shall see again "the
floor of heaven . . . thick inlaid with patines of bright
gold." But the miracle has not happened. Never in a
dozen years have I seen even one star really *shining*.
And since I see no chance of my ever leaving this place,
I must realize that only in memory or in imagination
will the night skies again declare to me the glory of
God.

But I am learning that what we call aging consists
in part in losing one lovely thing after another. I say
"in part," because it consists as well in gaining, whether
in earthly or heavenly treasure, or may do so. We are
fortunate, if the total gaining overbalances, or even coun-
terbalances, the total losing. But we must make up our
minds that, if we live long enough, and so far as earthly
wealth or what Gerard Manley Hopkins calls "leaves
[and] the things of man is concerned, the losing must
eventually preponderate." The substance of our earthly
life falls away bit by bit. Some of the bits do not greatly
matter, and of some perhaps we are glad to be relieved.
But most of them are good, and many are very precious.
Our friends make up a large part of that substance;
and one by one they depart, each leaving the empty
space larger behind him. Strangely enough, it was only
a few months ago I suddenly faced the fact that in all
probability I shall never see my sisters and brother
again, although none of them is very far away. By God's
grace and the gift of science, the voice need not yet

be still—and this is a great good—but the hand is as surely vanished as in death.

One may discern a mercy in all this. Human life at its richest is too rich to be all at once surrendered, although we know that too often it must be so. Perhaps those of us to whom it is given to live into old age may be fortunate in a way we do not always recognize. Our earthly life may have been so gradually impoverished that at the last we find ourselves able to relinquish it almost without pain.

I know that it is not always so. One may be so richly blest as still to hold, even at the end of a long life, some earthly treasure which seems to make up in value for all that one has lost. Such a one cannot escape the full pain of parting. But, even so, the years of gradual losing may have made it less hard to bear.

Let Not *My* Death Be Long

ONE WOULD BE INSENSITIVE indeed who did not thankfully recognize the great debt we owe to modern medical science in its having extended by many years the average span of human life. The greater part of this expansion is accounted for by its success in reducing infant mortality and in preventing, healing, or controlling certain diseases which have afflicted mankind, most of them from time immemorial. For these services there can be unqualified gratitude. But an incidental result of them creates serious problems, not only for individuals, but for society as well: in prolonging life, science has also prolonged death. And who can be grateful for *that?*

That this fact poses problems for society is obvious. The increased longevity would do so in itself. Since, so far as adults are concerned, most of the added years fall in the final post-retirement period of the average person's life, the proportion of persons in our population who have passed their "earning years" is ever growing, and the necessary public provision for aid becomes ever more expensive. But when consideration is given to the

further fact that of the time which science adds to the
elderly person's life no small part is often spent in total
disability and helplessness, mental as well as physical,
a condition entailing very special and extraordinarily
costly care—when consideration is given to *this* fact,
society's burden may be seen as unbearable, or as threat-
ening soon to become so. These facts create a problem
complex almost to the point of intractability; but society
must some time come realistically to grips with it.

When this happens, we must be prepared to accept
a solution which involves ending or drastically curtailing
the right to prolong death. The problem of determining
just when living ends and death begins is itself no easy
one, but it cannot, must not, prove insoluble. I have
pointed earlier in these pages to the manifest fact that
life and death are inextricably linked from our very
birth: when we begin to live we begin to die. But, even
if we live to old age, for the greater number of our
years the dominant element in this mixture is *life*, however much "labor and sorrow" there may be.

There comes a point for many of us, however, when
the balance shifts, at first perhaps ever so slightly but
eventually unmistakably and decisively. At that point
we are no longer both living and dying as is every
mortal thing; we are simply dying. If we are fully conscious (as most probably we shall not be), we shall know
and feel that this is true; and, according to every objective test, so in fact it is. When such is the case, no
one will deny that it is unnatural to prolong the dying.
But is it not also inhumane? I am not quite sure that
we should not, in some cases, be assisted to die. But
I *am* sure that the time comes in many a person's life

when he should be allowed to say, "Now lettest thou thy servant depart in peace," and to expect that man will not disregard and nullify God's merciful permission.

An American poet, otherwise unknown to me, Leonora Speyer, has written:

> Let not my death be long
> But light
> As a bird's singing;
> Happy decision in the height of song—
> Then flight
> From off the ultimate bough!
> And let my wing be strong,
> And my last note the first
> Of another's singing.
> See to it, Thou.

The last line is too imperious, particularly since men, not God, are most often responsible for the excessive lengths of our deaths. But with this reservation, who would not find these lines congenial and wish that it might be so with him?

Taking Death in Stride

I Received News a month ago of the death of a most
beloved friend—the dean of a Cambridge college, for-
merly the bishop of a London East End diocese, and
one of the most brilliant and productive theological
scholars of our time. More important than these and
many other distinctions: he was a wonderfully good
man—just and true, imaginatively generous, compas-
sionate, courageous, and as near to being pure in heart
as, I believe, a man can be. I have known him well
for more than thirty years, and have had no dearer
friend.

He was twenty years younger than I. Death came,
therefore, long before he had expected it; but it was
not in the usual sense sudden. He had been told by
his doctors that he could count on perhaps six months
to live, and that prediction was fulfilled almost to the
day. He wrote at the time of it that his first reaction
was one of shock (how else could it have been!), but
that this was soon followed by one of gratitude. He
did not agree at all, he said, with those who can speak

of a sudden death, as from a massive stroke or heart attack, as "a good way to die"; he was grateful for the advance notice. He thought: "Gosh! six months is a long time. One can do a lot in that. How am I going to use it?"

A little later he writes: " 'Preparing for death' is not the other-worldly, pious exercise stamped upon our hearts by Victorian sentimentality, a turning away from the things of earth to the things of heaven." He says it is really preparing, not for death at all, but "for eternal life, which means real living, more abundant life, begun, continued, but not ended, *now.*" Preparing for eternity thus means "learning really to live," "living it up," "giving the most to life and getting the most from it while it is on offer." This is why, he explains, he and his wife are then leaving for Venice and Florence, cities they have never seen and long have wanted to see. He writes, too, that he is giving what time and strength he can give each day to "all sorts of writing" he wants to finish. (Actually, before he died he had put into shape for publication two books and almost completed doing so for a third.)

Later still, he wrote: "The Christian takes his stand, not on optimism, but on hope. This is based not on rosy prognosis (from a human point of view mine is bleak), but, as St. Paul says, on suffering. This, he says, trains us to endure, and endurance brings proof that we have stood the test, and this proof is the ground of hope in the God who can bring resurrection out and through the other side of death."

Only today a letter came from his wife, written some weeks after his death and sent to a host of his friends.

She had stood at his side during the whole period of active waiting; and her love for him, her intelligence and understanding—not to speak of the complete freedom and honesty with which they were able mutually to share all their thoughts and feelings—undoubtedly helped immeasurably in making it the creative experience it was for him, and for her. This brief record of a most remarkable death would not be even summarily complete if I did not quote from one of the paragraphs of her letter. After describing in simple but moving terms her husband's last months, weeks and days, the circumstances of his quiet death, and the beautiful funeral and burial services in the village church and graveyard near their Yorkshire home—services marked less by grief than by a solemn joy—she writes:

. . . To be told that one has six months to live does not condemn one to six months of misery unless we allow it to do so. It is not death but the fear of death that can destroy us. . . . John decided to take responsibility for his dying; he accepted without fretting the limitations it imposed on him and was therefore able to use his resources to the full for the work he considered realistically within his scope. He somehow managed to take death in his stride, preparing for it with the same efficiency and clarity of mind as he did for any absence from home. Death was simply another engagement he had to keep. But what this six months has shown us above all is that this is not an exploration to be undertaken alone. When our friends are prepared to face it with us our dying can teach us to live.

Hope *Also* *Abides*

WHAT IS UNDOUBTEDLY ST. PAUL'S BEST KNOWN SINGLE UTTERANCE is also perhaps the most significant: "And now abide faith, hope, love, these three, and the greatest of these is love." This is not a casual utterance. It is not, as many regard it, merely an effective rhetorical flourish at the end of an extraordinarily elequent passage. On the contrary, it is a careful, deliberate statement based on thoughtful critical reflection on his own experience. Traditionally "these three" have been called "the three virtues." But unless the word "virtues" is being used in a quite unusual sense, that phrase does not apply. If "virtues," why "these three" only?, one may ask. Are there not many virtues equally "abiding"— why not honesty, patience, humility, courage? And, one may further ask, are love, faith, hope properly called "virtues" at all? No, we must say; Paul is not speaking of moral excellences. He is speaking of the fundamental structural elements, essential and irreducible, of what he sees as our true life as persons.

What sets "these three" off from what are properly

called "virtues," important as these are, is the largely "adjectival" character of the latter. "Courage," "humility," "honesty" and the like are abstractions, the names we give to certain moral characteristics a person may possess. "Courage" means much the same thing as the quality of being courageous; "humility," as unpretentiousness; "honesty," as trustworthiness. But love, faith and hope, as Paul is thinking of them, are more objective, substantive terms, far more concrete in meaning. "Love" is not the quality of being generally loving, although this may be implied; "faith" is not having the virtue of loyalty, nor is "hope" mere hopefulness, an habitually optimistic attitude toward the future. As he means to be understood, the "love" is God's love for us, indeed for all his creation—an objective thing "poured out" in such abundance especially, as Paul feels it, in Christ. "Faith" is our openness to this love, our acceptance of it, our letting it fill and overflow our hearts. With "these two," many, even many Christians, would say, Paul could, and therefore should, have stopped. Love and faith, when given their full, true meaning for him, say it all. But Paul manifestly does not feel so. In the new life of the Spirit, whose basic and essential structure he is very carefully delineating, there is a third element which he finds he cannot leave out. In this conviction that hope cannot be omitted, Christian experience over all the centuries has amply borne him out.

For it is simply a matter of fact that we cannot trust the love of God to the point of giving ourselves up to it without finding ourselves possessed of an indefeasible, invincible hope—a conviction, both intuitive and logical, that nothing can separate us from this love; that there is a Sovereign Goodness which will not let go its hold upon us, despite our sin and our folly, despite our doubt and unbelief; a Goodness which will accompany us through our tears, through the failure of our physical and mental powers, through our dying, and at the last will lead us into the experience of what this same love has prepared for us.

What this same Love has prepared for us—that is the content of our hope, and we can know that this is "more than we can ask or think." We shall be wise if we do not seek or expect any more definite or specific knowledge of it, for our experience offers no ground for such knowledge. Do you ask, writes Paul: "How are the dead raised up? with what body do they come?" His rejoinder is that we are foolish to ask that kind of question. William Temple is quoted as saying that of nothing was he more sure than of life after death, "but [he said] I do not have any idea of what it will be like, and I am glad I do not, for I know my idea would be wrong." Such, in the very nature of the case, it must obviously be, and we should not expect, or even want, it to be other. We must trust the Love which gives us the only firm ground of our hope to fulfill it in its own perfectly appropriate way.

The Last *S*urprise

HERMAN MELVILLE SPEAKS SOMEWHERE of "Stoics astounded into heaven." I can think of two friends whose deaths have occurred recently and of whom this might be said, although I do not believe either of them would have classified himself as a Stoic. Indeed, when I reflect on the matter, I can recall many whom I have known long since and lost awhile who must have found themselves in heaven only to their great surprise. One of the spirituals tells us that many who are talking about heaven aren't going there. That may or may not be true; but the converse, I am sure, *is* true: many who aren't talking about heaven *are* going there.

And how could it be otherwise? Our immortality is either a fact or it is not. Its factualness does not depend at all on what we may think or believe about it. The same can be said of the love of God which assures our immortality by refusing to loosen its hold upon us— this love does not cease to be because we do not acknowledge it. According to Jesus, not everyone who says, "Lord, Lord," is as ready as he thinks to enter the kingdom of heaven. But, again, the converse of this remark must be just as surely true: Many who have never said, "Lord, Lord," may at the last, and to their great astonishment, hear the Lord say, "Come, ye blessed of my Father; inherit the kingdom prepared for you from the foundation of the world."

Too often we think of ourselves more highly than we ought to think. This is a grievous fault and—who knows?—some time, somewhere we may have grievously to answer for it. But there is such a thing as putting too low a valuation on one's worth and taking too modest a view of one's destiny. And this, as often as not, is true of the most honorable and courageous, the most humane and generous, the most sensitively perceptive, of men and women.

Christmas and Easter

IT IS NOT STRANGE that Christmas and Easter are the two great festivals of Christianity, because they represent the two truths—or the two aspects of a single truth—which are at its heart. Between them, as between the poles of a vital circuit, all that is significant and alive in the Christian experience moves. Sometimes attempts are made to separate them, to exclude the meaning of either Christmas or Easter; but when such attempts succeed, the living current is broken. Christmas means the humanness of God, his nearness to man; Easter means the divineness of man, his nearness to God. Together they mean the infinite significance of human life in an infinitely significant world.

It is hardly necessary to emphasize the fact that Christmas does symbolize the nearness of God—this meaning is too much a part of our experience. Then is the time when friendships are most precious, the world most strangely beautiful, and faith in God almost a simple thing. Never does the wonder of life seem so intimately present as at Christmas. It is the most gracious and blessed of the year's days for it is the celebration of the pervasive involvement of the ultimate mystery in all that makes up our ordinary experience, the immanence of God, the Word made flesh.

The stories which early sprang up around the birth of Jesus unconsciously express this same meaning. An angel appears to some shepherds and a multitude of the heavenly host sing a hymn never heard before on land or sea; a star drops low from the skies to guide three magi from distant unknown lands to the little Judean village; while in a stable in the arms of a poor Galilean mother God himself lies a tiny babe. Never has the faraway been brought so near, and matters so sublime been placed in a setting so homely and ordinary. It would seem absurdly irrelevant to ask if these stories are true. Of course they are—not because they happened once (it does not matter whether they did or not)— but because they are always happening. He to whom the world without and within is only an object of thoughtless sensation or even of thoughtful scrutiny, will not believe them. But he to whom life is replete with mystery, to whom the world is a perpetual call to wonder and worship, who has himself heard angels singing at dawn or has seen a halo about the head of some child— he will not think of denying. For him the scene at Bethlehem is a timeless representation of the transcendent importance of human life because God has identified himself with it. The divine has become human; the dayspring from on high has visited us; God has come to dwell with men.

But if Christmas celebrates the condescension of the divine, Easter speaks of the exaltation of the human.

If Christmas shows us God as a little child, Easter shows us man standing to his full moral stature and, if only after unspeakable struggle and agony ("even the death of the Cross"), victorious over all his enemies and raised to God's right hand. For the resurrection of Christ, like his birth, is not a mere event in the past; it is the symbol of an eternal fact: Man was made in the image of God and will not be allowed to fail in the end to realize his true nature and destiny. Divinity is not merely above him and around him; it is also within him—indeed, it is the very essence of his inmost self.

Thus in Christmas and Easter God and man are fully met. The separation between the natural and the supernatural is done away. The old heaven and earth are no more; a new heaven and earth, in which the one is merged with the other, has come into being. As poetry is to the poem or music to the song, as the vision of the artist is to the masterpiece which embodies it, so the Ultimate Truth, Beauty, Love—the Reality of God— is to the universe, in which it finds not only its glorious expression, but, so far as we can know, its very identity. Every common bush is afire with God. And just as we see revealed in the nature about us the Beauty of God, so we may hope that through God's mercy and man's own struggle humanity too will become the image of his glory.

"Come, let us live the poetry we sing," Edwin Markham has written. Christmas and Easter are genuine parts of the poetry of our race. Like all such poetry they are true, but they will not be fully true until we write them into our lives and the life of our world. But we have not arranged our world and we do not conduct its affairs on the assumption that every man is a child of God and has in him immeasurable possibilities for growth in goodness and wisdom. We have worshiped the baby of the woman of Bethlehem but we have forgotten the babies of the millions of women who throng the alleys of our cities. We have stood with adoration at the empty tomb of Jesus but we have denied in a thousand ways the immortality of our brothers.

Come, we who sing of a poor woman's Child born with a strange halo about his head and of a carpenter's Son who sits at the right hand of the throne of God, let us live the poetry we sing!

Only to Be Remembered?

One of My Dearest Friends Has Died, a remarkably good and gifted person, and I have just now returned from a memorial service in which her extraordinarily beautiful and useful life was celebrated. The service was attended by her husband and children and by a host of friends. Tribute was paid to her—tribute as nearly adequate as, I dare say, any of us could have put into words. We were reminded of her integrity, her energy of will, her firmness in what she saw as right and true, her sharp and well-informed intelligence, her uncompromising honesty in small matters and large, her keen discernment and vigorous rejection of all humbug and hypocrisy, her simplicity and the absence of all pretentiousness, her eager generosity, her wide-ranging human interests and sympathies crossing all national boundaries, her freedom from prejudices which would separate her from persons of other races and cultures, her humility and readiness to acknowledge her own mistakes, faults, and failures, her tolerance and her sensitivity to the sensibilities of others, her love of beauty, her never-failing sense of humor, her uncomplaining patience under suffering or disappointment. . . . And all of this we recognized to be true. She was indeed all of this, and more. *So* we knew her, and *so* we shall always remember her.

But now I find myself asking: Is this the end? Does she, now and hereafter, live only in our memories of her or in the continuing influence of her life—"a good diffused" in a "world made better by her presence," to use George Eliot's noble phrases?

I know that I must say more than this, not because I so much want to, but because I should find the universe intolerably irrational if I could not. Wordsworth suggests that "our birth is but a sleep and a forgetting": and in very truth it may be so. But more obviously and surely is it true that our birth is an *awakening.* Our death, too, is a sleep and a forgetting, but who can say that here again there is not also an awakening? When I think of such a life as Dorothea's, my mind boggles and my heart revolts at any denial of it. How can it be that something so beautifully wrought and bearing in itself the very image of its Maker should have been made only to be destroyed? I refuse, and find it impossible, to believe it can be so. For all the apparently wasteful extravagance of his creation, I cannot believe that God is so prodigal of his dearest treasures as not to have, even now, my beloved friend safely in his keeping.

The Parting Guest

"THERE IS A TIME TO DIE," writes the worldly-wise author
of Ecclesiastes. He is undoubtedly speaking as a fatal-
ist—there is a predetermined time for the death of each
of us. With that idea of his, most of us, I feel sure,
would disagree. But still the phrase "time to die" may
have meaning for us. We often feel that someone has
died before his time and, again often, that for someone
the "time to die" has long since passed. In cases of
the one kind death seems, from our human point of
view, a cruel interruption; in cases of the other kind,
a rest and liberation too long delayed. But there is so
fortunate a thing as death's arriving at a time appropriate
and altogether good—our work done, our presence (although no doubt very dear to those who love us) no
longer greatly needed by anyone, our energies rapidly
diminishing, our senses beginning to fail, our strength
no longer equal to the demands of life, and yet alert
enough in mind to be gratefully aware that life has
given us love and beauty in value far in excess of any
price we have been asked to pay. When all of this is

146

true, may it not be time to die? We may not be able always to recognize this fact about ourselves, and it may be hard sometimes to recognize it as true for someone we love. But may it not be true?

One of James Whitcomb Riley's poems is called, "A Parting Guest":

> What delightful hosts are they,
>   Life and love!
> Lingeringly I turn away
> This late hour, yet glad enough
>   They have not withheld from me
>   Their high hospitality.
> So with face lit with delight
>   And all gratitude I stay
>   Yet to shake their hand and say,
> "Thanks. So fine a time. Good-night."

If, like me, you find this little poem appealing, it is most obviously because it describes very simply and truly and with a certain poignant charm what we recognize as the appropriate way to accept death—at any rate, one's own death—especially if life has been long and rewarding. It is true that one can never escape entirely the sadness of farewell—*"lingeringly* I turn away this late hour"—but, even so, death is accepted willingly, even cheerfully. It is good if one can die so.

But the poem holds another truth, less obvious but perhaps more important: the final "Good-night" marks the parting of a *guest*. Human life and love have been our generous and delightful *hosts* for a while, and we are loath to leave them; but the evening is far spent and it is time to go. How we left home for our visit and by what route we came, we have, strange to say, forgotten; and the way of our return we do not, even dimly, know: but, thanking our kind hosts, we step into the darkness without fear. For we are going *home*, and we know that a Gentle Hand—but very Strong and Sure—is waiting in the still night to lead us there.

Acknowledgments

THE SOURCES OF QUOTED MATERIAL in this book are usually identified in the text, but often I have not troubled the reader or myself by naming works or authors when quotations are so familiar as to require no identification. Some of them, especially from the Bible and Shakespeare, I have often not even set out as such. It may not be amiss, however, to say that the stanza quoted on p. 31 is the last stanza of Sidney Lanier's fine poem, "The Marshes of Glynn," that the quoted lines on p. 115 are from Edward Fitzgerald's "The Rubaiyat of Omar Khayyam." The stanza found on p. 58 I remember as having been written by Nietzsche (but I have not been able to verify the attribution).

As to certain other literary allusions, I may say that A. E. Housman's description of the origin of one of his lyrics (p. 73) may be found in his *The Name and Nature of Poetry* (Cambridge University Press) and that the essay of Gilbert Chesterton which is commented on in two of the pieces is entitled, "The Furrows" and appears in *Alarms and Discursions* (Dodd, Mead, and

Company). The quotation from Havelock Ellis on p. 33 is from *The Dance of Life* (Houghton Mifflin Company). The article cited on p. 86 was published in *The Christian Century*.

The single line from Edna St. Vincent Millay quoted at the beginning of this book, and from which its title is derived, is from her poem "God's World" in her *Collected Poems* (Harper and Row, Copyright 1917, 1945). It is used by permission of Norma Millay Ellis, Miss Millay's literary executor.

For the quotations on pp. 51 and 134 I have received personal permission from the authors.

In the Foreword I mentioned the fact that in a few of the essays I have used small bits of earlier writings of mine, abridged, expanded, or otherwise adapted to new purposes. In that connection I have in mind particularly two paragraphs in *The Ethic of Jesus in the Teaching of the Church* (Abingdon Press); three paragraphs in *Never Far from Home* (Word, Inc.); a page or two in my essay in *The Christian Answer*, edited by H. P. Van Dusen (Charles Scribner's Sons); and one paragraph in my essay in *The Gospel, the Church and the World*, edited by K. S. Latourette (Harper and Brothers).

J. K.

Dr. John Knox had his first article published in *The Christian Century* in 1929 and has been frequently published in leading Christian journals ever since. In addition to writing several books, he has also served as the editor of *The Journal of Religion* and *Religion and the Present Crisis*. He was Associate Editor of New Testament and Exegesis for *The Interpreter's Bible* and *The Interpreter's Dictionary of the Bible*. He served as Baldwin Professor of Sacred Literature at Union Seminary and Professor of New Testament at Episcopal Theological Seminary of the Southwest. He received the B.A. in Classics at Randolph-Macon College, the B.D. in New Testament from Candler School of Theology, Emory University, and the Ph.D. in New Testament from the University of Chicago. He was also awarded a D.D. degree by the Philadelphia Divinity School, and the S.T.D. from both General Theological Seminary and Berkeley Divinity School. He also served terms as President of the American Theological Society and the Society of Biblical Literature.